EMILY'S CHALLENGE
AND OTHER BROWNIE STORIES

Emily was sitting at the kitchen table writing invitations. In six days time she would be eight and her mum had said she could have a birthday party. She was excited.

She signed her name very carefully on the last five invitations – to the members of her Brownie Six. It was very important that Linda, Karen, Jill, Helen and Sue got the right message. The party would be miserable if they didn't turn up.

'There. That's the lot.' With a sigh of relief she put down the pen.

Her mum flicked through the pile of envelopes. 'No it isn't. You've forgotten Denise.'

Emily groaned. She didn't like her cousin Denise. Denise had nothing to say. Worse still, she was allergic to dogs, so whenever she came to visit, Nipper had to go outside. How could Emily enjoy her party if Denise came?

Also available from Knight Books:

Amy's Promise and Other Brownie stories

Emily's Challenge and Other Brownie Stories

---

by Lynda Neilands
Illustrated by Jenny Mumford

KNIGHT BOOKS
Hodder and Stoughton

Text copyright © 1992 by the Girl Guides
Association
Illustrations copyright © 1992 by Jenny
Mumford

First published in Great Britain in
this collection by Knight Books in 1992

All these stories have previously appeared
in the *Brownie* magazine.

Printed and bound in Great Britain for
Hodder and Stoughton Children's Books a
division of Hodder and Stoughton Ltd.,
Mill Road, Dunton Green, Sevenoaks, Kent
TN13 2YA. (Editorial Office: 47 Bedford
Square, London WC1B 3DP) by Clays Ltd,
St Ives plc. Photoset by Rowland
Phototypesetting Ltd., Bury St Edmunds,
Suffolk.

A CIP catalogue record for this book is
available from the British Library

ISBN 0-340-58003-8

Contents

Emily's Challenge

Emily was sitting at the kitchen table writing invitations. In six days time she would be eight and her mum had said she could have a birthday party. She was excited. Very excited. It was hard to feel excited and write clearly at the same time. The last three letters of her name kept running into each other.

'It looks as if you've signed yourself Emu,' her mum pointed out. 'An emu is a large Australian bird. Your friends will think they've been invited to a birthday party in the zoo.'

Emily giggled but she signed her name very carefully on the last five invitations – to the members of her Brownie Six. It was very important that Linda, Karen, Jill, Helen and Sue got the right message. The party would be miserable if they didn't turn up.

'There. That's the lot.' With a sigh of relief she put down the pen and wiggled her hand backwards and forwards.

Her mum flicked through the pile of envelopes, 'No it isn't. You've forgotten Denise.'

'Denise! Oh Mum!' Emily groaned. She didn't like Denise. Denise wore her hair in two straggly plaits and had nothing to say. Worse still, she was allergic to dogs. Dogs made Denise sneeze, which meant that whenever she came to visit, Emily's mum tied Nipper to the clothesline in the back yard.

'Please Mum, don't make me invite her,' Emily pleaded.

Mrs Martin handed her daughter the pen. 'Denise is your cousin. It would hurt Auntie Ann's feelings if we left her out.'

Secretly, for the rest of the week, Emily hoped that Auntie Ann would misread the invitation and take Denise to the zoo by mistake, but she didn't. At two o'clock on Saturday afternoon Denise and Auntie Ann arrived – a whole three quarters of an hour earlier than expected. Auntie Ann said she had something important to ask Emily's mother and went into the kitchen.

'Hello, Denise,' Emily tried to sound friendly. 'It's all right. You don't have to sneeze. Nipper's already outside.'

Denise nodded without saying anything, handed Emily a parcel and sat down on the edge of an armchair.

Eagerly Emily fingered the present. It felt generally soft with a hard centre. Could it be a tiny doll wrapped in a blanket? That would be brilliant. She tore off the paper to find two pairs of school socks wrapped round a bottle of bath salts.

'Thanks, Denise,' she said politely.

Denise nodded again, still without speaking.

Fortunately, at that moment the twins from next door came in. Then Sue arrived, followed by Linda and Jill, and soon the party was in full swing, with music and games and the smell of cocktail sausages sizzling in the oven, and all sorts of presents you couldn't use in the bath.

'This is my best birthday ever,' Emily hugged herself in excitement. After she had blown out the candles on her cake, while everyone else was getting ready to go home, Mrs Martin called her into the kitchen.

There was a very firm look on her face.

'I've something to tell you, Emily,' she said, 'and I don't want any complaints.'

Emily shifted uneasily from foot to foot. What could it be?

Her mother's next words sent her bolting out of the back door to bury her face in Nipper's wire-haired coat. It wasn't fair. The whole day had been ruined and the next few weeks were going to be miserable.

'Auntie Ann and Uncle Tom have to go away on business,' her mum had explained, 'so Denise is coming to stay here.'

On Monday afternoon Uncle Tom brought Denise and two enormous suitcases round to the house. As they came into the hall the kitchen door opened and Nipper bounded up. Denise squealed. Mrs Martin immediately grabbed the terrier by the scruff of the neck and threw him outside into the rain.

'Don't, Mum! That's cruel! He'll get soaked,' Emily cried.

'No he won't. He'll go into the shed,' said her mum. But Emily knew that Nipper hated the shed.

While her mum and Denise were upstairs unpacking, she sneaked Nipper through the back door into the living room and made him lie behind the chair.

'You've got to stay still,' she warned, covering the chair back with her anorak so that nobody would see he was there. Then she got a jigsaw puzzle out of the toy cupboard and tipped the pieces on to the rug.

'Have you ever done a jigsaw like this?' Emily asked Denise as she came into the room. It was of a man in a rowing boat. Denise shook her head, 'I don't do jigsaws,' she muttered.

Emily spent the next half an hour happily sorting bits of sea into one pile and bits of sky into another. She was about to begin a bits-of-boat pile when Mrs Martin poked her head round the door.

'Everything all right, girls?' she asked. Then she frowned, 'Emily, you know you're meant to hang your coat in the hall. What's it doing on the chair?'

Emily bit her lip. 'I don't know, Mum,' she said, without looking up.

'Go and hang it up now,' said Mrs Martin, 'makes the room look untidy.' She whipped the coat off the chair. 'Ah, now I see the real reason!' There was Nipper – sitting up and scratching.

'Auntie Margaret! Auntie Margaret! Emily didn't do what she was told!' Denise wailed. 'Atchoo!' She sneezed so hard that the sky-pile collapsed.

'Now look what you've done,' snapped Emily.

'That's enough, Emily!' said Mrs Martin. 'Any more of this silliness and I'll send you to bed – which means you miss Brownies.'

The last thing Emily wanted was to miss Brownies. Her Six were practising a puppet show to perform the following week.

'I'm sorry, Mum.' She gathered up the pieces.

As soon as Mrs Martin had hauled Nipper out of the room, Denise found her tongue.

'Dogs are stupid,' she said.

'No they aren't,' said Emily, carefully rebuilding the sky-pile.

'Jigsaws are stupid,' said Denise.

Emily glared at her. 'Oh yes? I suppose everything I like is stupid. I suppose Brownies are stupid too?'

'That's right,' Denise nodded, 'Brownies are stupid.'

It was the last straw. 'Brownies are not stupid,' shouted Emily, 'but you are. You're the stupidest person I know.'

'Auntie Margaret! Auntie Margaret! Emily said I was stupid,' Denise wailed.

Emily arrived in the Brownie hall that evening with none of her usual bounce.

'What's the matter with you?' asked Linda, her Sixer.

'It's my cousin. Remember, the girl with straggly plaits you met at my party. She's making my life miserable.' And out came the whole story.

When Emily had finished, Linda looked at her thoughtfully. 'You know what? I think this is a great chance for a Mind Your Tongue Challenge.'

Emily frowned. 'What's that?'

'It's one of the Do Your Best Challenges on the Brownie Road. Why not challenge yourself not to say anything nasty to Denise for the rest of her visit?'

'Gosh, I couldn't!' Emily gasped.

'Yes, you could. It wouldn't be easy, but real Challenges never are,' said Linda with a knowing smile. 'Now come on, we'd better join the rest, we're already five minutes late for the practice.'

'I've challenged myself to do something really difficult this week,' Emily told her mum next morning over breakfast. Denise was still upstairs in the bathroom.

'Oh, what's that?'

'I can't say, just in case it doesn't work.' Emily poured herself a bowl of cornflakes.

She was spooning honey on to her toast, when Denise came in.

'There you are at last! We were beginning to think you'd washed yourself down the plug-hole,' her tongue almost said. She minded it just in time, smiled stickily, and said, 'You should try some of this honey, Denise, it's great!'

This was a good beginning. Two spoonfuls of honey later, she looked at her watch and felt more pleased with herself than ever. She hadn't said anything nasty to Denise for a whole ten minutes.

'Can we go to the pool after school today?' she asked as they left the table. She was practising for her Brownie Swimmer badge and often went swimming on a Wednesday.

Mrs Martin considered. 'Do you want to go swimming, Denise?'

'No,' said Denise. 'I don't like swimming.'

'That's not . . .' Emily was about to say, 'That's not fair!' but she managed to change it to, 'That's not a problem! What do you like doing, Denise?'

Her cousin looked at her in amazement. 'I like reading,' she said in a small voice.

'So do I,' said Emily. 'Tell you what, we'll go to the library after school. OK?'

'OK,' said Denise and for the first time since coming to stay she smiled.

As the week went on Emily kept minding her tongue and Denise smiled more and more. She talked more too. She was fun to be with when she smiled and talked, Emily discovered. By Saturday afternoon she had even started to help with the jigsaw puzzle.

They only had twenty more pieces to fit into place, when Mrs Martin brought Linda into the room.

Emily was delighted to see her Sixer but one look at Linda's face told her that something had gone wrong.

'We'll have to cancel the puppet show,' the older girl said sadly. 'Helen fell off her pony this morning and banged her head. She's all right but Dr Miller says she's to stay at home until Wednesday and we can't put on the show without her.'

What a disappointment! Emily had been looking forward to working the Fairy Godmother in the puppet show for months. And poor Helen! How awful to be stuck indoors! Emily could feel her chin wobbling. She didn't know whether it was because of what had happened to Helen, or because the show had been cancelled.

Suddenly she realised that Denise was looking at her with an odd expression on her face – as if she wanted to say something but wasn't sure how to begin.

'Maybe . . . maybe . . . I could help?' she stammered, 'maybe I could take Helen's place?'

The puppet show went ahead after all.

Denise worked the Prince Charming puppet and said Helen's lines as if she'd been practising them for months.

'That was great! I'd no idea you'd be so good!' Emily told her afterwards.

'Neither did I.' Thoughtfully, Denise twisted the end of one plait round her finger. 'You know, up to now I've never wanted to try anything new

in case I looked stupid, but staying with you has made me feel different. I don't even think I'd mind if Nipper came in now.'

'Let's find out,' Emily beamed.

She brought Nipper into the living room and held him tightly on her lap while her cousin slotted the final pieces of the jigsaw in place. Who would have thought that minding her tongue would work out so brilliantly! It seemed almost too good to be true. The picture was complete at last and Denise hadn't sneezed once!

Sophie Strikes Again

It was Christmas Eve. Emily tossed and turned in her bed. Getting to sleep on Christmas Eve was always hard, but this year it seemed impossible. It was such a *special* Christmas. First, and most importantly, her dad was home from the North Sea and secondly she had done her Christmas shopping all by herself.

'Christmas is a time when Brownies should do their best to make other people happy,' Mrs James, her Guider, had said. Emily had remembered that as she went around Allsorts Department Store. There were four people she planned to make happy: her dad, her mum, Sophie and one of the elderly ladies who lived in Riversdale House.

Riversdale House was the old people's home beside the Brownie hall and the Brownies took presents there every Christmas.

'I bet the old lady who opens the parcel I bought will get a surprise,' Emily thought. She hadn't just bought one thing, but two: something pretty and something useful – a lace handkerchief and a hairnet.

She had two things each for her mum, dad and Sophie too. Their neatly labelled presents lay under the Christmas tree wrapped in kitchen roll (she hadn't been able to afford wrapping paper) waiting for the morning.

If *only* the morning would come soon. Emily wriggled around for another three quarters of an hour and finally fell asleep. She dreamed she was unwrapping a present of her own – a huge cardboard box with a real live pony snorting and kicking inside. Then she dreamed she was trying to ride it and it wouldn't stop whinnying.

Suddenly she realised that whinnying noise was her alarm clock ringing beside her bed. Seven o'clock. With a thrill of delight she threw back the duvet and ran across the hall to her sister's room. 'It's morning, Sophie,' she squealed as she ran. 'Happy Christmas!'

But Sophie's bed was empty. 'She must be downstairs already,' Emily thought, racing down the stairs. 'She'll be in big trouble if she's opening anything. She knows she's not allowed . . .'

Sure enough Sophie was under the Christmas tree. But she wasn't opening presents. Just poking them. She had been fingering the parcels all

week. She was allowed to do that as long as she didn't tear the paper or squeeze too hard.

'All right, Sophie. You'll be able to see what's inside the minute Mum and Dad get up.'

No sooner had Emily spoken the words, than Mr and Mrs Martin arrived in the living room in their dressing gowns, looking bleary-eyed but cheerful.

'Happy Christmas, darlings,' Mrs Martin sank on to the settee.

'Well, well, what's this I see? A present with *my* name on the label,' Mr Martin dived under the tree. 'And look, here's one for Mum, and this one's for Sophie.'

'That's right,' said Emily proudly. 'They're from me.'

'So what have we here?' Her father unwound the kitchen roll eagerly. 'Well I never!' He sounded puzzled, then started to laugh. 'Tights and eye-shadow. Just what I wanted.'

'That's for Mum! You've opened the wrong one.' Emily snatched the parcel out of his hands.

'It had my name on the label. Look, "DAD". That's what it says.'

Before Emily could even glance at the label, her mum discovered a tie-pin and shaving foam in her parcel. 'What's in yours, Sophie?' she called.

Sophie didn't say anything. She just held up a grey hairnet in one hand and a white hanky in the other and beamed.

'Oh no! I bought those to take to Riversdale House. The labels are all mixed up,' Emily groaned.

Her dad seemed to find the whole thing terribly funny. He could hardly speak for laughing. 'So if Sophie has a . . . hanky and a hairnet . . . what's . . . the Riversdale lady . . . got?' he choked.

'Gosh!' Emily turned purple with horror. At that very moment in Riversdale House some senior citizen was opening a parcel meant for a three-year-old child. It would seem like a joke . . . or even worse . . . an insult! She clutched her mother's sleeve. 'I'll have to go over to the home right away and explain, Mum. Otherwise the matron might think I did it on purpose and the Brownies won't be invited back next year.'

Mrs Martin nodded. 'You can take the bath salts Auntie Ann gave me,' she said. 'It's still early, so the ladies probably haven't even opened their presents yet. Just ask the matron to exchange gifts.'

Now Mr Martin saw the serious side to it too and offered to give Emily a lift.

'I just hope we're in time,' Emily muttered as they zoomed down the road.

Two minutes later they were driving up to Riversdale House. Mrs Blunt, the matron, greeted them at the door.

Emily had had a little speech of apology all prepared but one look at Mrs Blunt and the words went completely out of her head. Was she seeing things? She glanced up at her dad. Yes, his lips were twitching. He'd seen it too. Mrs Blunt's pink powdery face had been painted with a big black twirly moustache.

Emily couldn't help herself. She started to giggle.

'Well, as you can see, we've been having some fun and games here,' the matron smiled. 'Miss Cook, in room nine, got a box of jelly babies and a packet of face paints as her Brownie gift. She's been having a wonderful time with them. The Brownie who thought of it deserves a thank you badge.'

Emily had to be honest. 'Well, umm, I'm the Brownie, but actually it was a mistake. I bought the face paints for my little sister only she went and mixed up the labels on all my Christmas gifts so Miss Cook got the wrong thing . . .'

'Oh dear,' sighed Mrs Blunt. 'I suppose this means you want them back?'

'Oh no. Not now that I know they're making Miss Cook happy.'

'But what about your little sister, she'll be disappointed.'

'No. She doesn't mind. She's turned Miss Cook's present into a hammock and a sheet for her doll.'

'Well, it looks as if everything's worked out perfectly then,' smiled Mrs Blunt.

Emily thought so too – until she got home. Her dad handed her a present with her name on the

front and it turned out to be a large packet of dog biscuits.

'Sophie strikes again,' he grinned. 'I suppose you'd better swap with Nipper. You'll find his present behind the settee.'

What Emily found behind the settee was a super, fantastic, brand-new bike.

'I'll never forget this Christmas,' she gasped. 'It's the funniest, happiest, specialest day of my life.'

The Garden Shed Mystery

Christmas was over. The tree and the cards had come down. Life was back to normal. School . . . homework . . . Brownies . . .

'Please, Mum, are there any more fish fingers?'

Emily sat at the kitchen table eating her tea.

'You want *more*!' Her mother looked at her in astonishment. 'Last week you told me you didn't like fish fingers . . .'

'I don't.' Emily wrinkled her nose. 'But I've made a New Year's resolution to eat every sort of food without complaining.' She held out her plate virtuously. 'And I'm still hungry.'

In the hallway the telephone rang. 'Help yourself. There are a few extra under the grill.' Mrs Martin nodded towards the cooker on her way through the door.

A few moments later she was back. 'That was Mrs James. She's painting her bathroom ceiling and wants to borrow the old bedspread we keep in the garden shed. She'll pick you up for Brownies when she comes to collect it.'

A look of horror crossed Emily's face. 'Oh, Mum, why couldn't she borrow a bedspread from somebody else?' she wailed. 'We *need* ours . . .'

'Whatever for?'

'Well . . . for . . . for . . . *sitting* on. The shed floor is so hard and cold. And you always say that sitting on hard cold floors can give you a chill. Please . . . let me ring Mrs James and tell her you've changed your mind.'

'Don't be ridiculous. You can sit on something else. There are plenty of old cushions and rugs.' Mrs Martin rummaged through a drawer. 'That's funny,' she muttered. 'I can't seem to find the shed key. Have you seen it?'

'It was in the drawer,' Emily sat very still, frowning at her empty plate.

'Well it's gone now. Quick! Help me look. Mrs James will be here in a few minutes . . .'

Still frowning, Emily joined the search, opening cupboards, pulling out saucepans, taking the lids off biscuit tins.

'There's no need to get carried away,' her mother frowned as Emily climbed on to a chair and began to run her fingers along the curtain rail. 'Keys don't build nests, you know.'

'Perhaps it got mixed into that apple tart,'

Emily pointed down to the golden brown pie on top of the cooker. 'Would you like me to cut a slice and poke around inside?'

'No I would not.' Mrs Martin sat down with a sigh and poured herself a cup of tea. 'You've done quite enough looking for the time being.' Thoughtfully she reached for the milk jug. 'Stop pulling the place apart, Emily, and get me some milk. I need to think . . .'

Emily went over to the fridge. 'Um . . . there isn't any,' she said in a small voice.

'What! But there was a full carton there this afternoon. Don't tell me that's disappeared too!'

'Um . . . it isn't here now.'

'I can't believe this!' Her mother shook her head. 'First the key . . . now the milk. What's going to vanish next?'

She was still sitting in her chair, sipping black tea and looking bewildered when Mrs James arrived.

'Happy New Year, Margaret,' the dark-haired Guider cried cheerfully. 'Emily, if you're ready, we'll be on our way. Thanks a million for the loan of the bedspread. If you can just tell me where it is I'll put it into the boot of the car.'

'Well . . . er . . . actually there's been a bit of a problem.' Mrs Martin set her cup down and explained about the missing key.

Mrs James was so used to viewing problems as challenges she immediately came up with an idea. 'I have dozens of different keys on my key-ring,' she said. 'Perhaps one of them would fit the lock . . .'

'Yes, but there isn't time to check now.' Emily marched towards the door trailing her anorak behind. 'We might run into a traffic jam on the way to Brownies, and then we'd be kept . . . Oh no! Bad dog, Nipper. Drop! Drop!'

Nipper had pounced on the coat and pulled it from her grasp. Before Emily's horrified gaze, he shook it backwards and forwards like a rat, scattering the contents of the pockets in all directions. A stick of chewing gum shot on to the pedal bin. A ten pence piece hit the door of the cooker. And a flat kitchen-roll parcel landed with a thud at Mrs James's feet.

Grrrr. Nipper attacked it.

'BAD DOG!' Something about his mistress's tone told the terrier the game was over. His tail drooped and he slunk back into his basket, dragging the kitchen roll beside him, leaving the contents of the parcel behind. There they lay on the tiles, part shrivelled, part gleaming.

Four fish fingers and a small metallic key.

Emily's mother bent over. She picked up the shed key and examined it silently. 'Just *what* is

the meaning of this?' she cried in a voice full of anger and surprise.

'I'm sorry. I'm really sorry,' the girl started to cry. 'But you don't understand what it's like . . . To think you have a family that loves you . . . and then to discover you're just a nuisance . . . and they couldn't care less whether you live or die!' And, snatching the key from her mother's palm, she ran out through the back door.

Mrs Martin looked more bewildered than ever. 'We'd better find out what that was about,' she said to Mrs James.

They found Emily in the garden shed, huddled on the bedspread, her arms round her legs and her head buried between her knees – the picture of misery.

'Oh, darling!' Mrs Martin sounded as if she was about to cry herself. 'How could you *ever* imagine we didn't love you . . .'

Emily stopped sniffing. 'I wasn't talking about *me*,' she said sharply.

Even as she spoke, a small fluffy head poked out under her chin.

'A kitten!' Mrs Martin gasped.

Wriggle. Dart. The little ball of orange fur swung down Emily's sweat pants on to the floor and pranced sideways.

'I found him today . . . on the way home from

school . . . in a ditch at the side of the road . . . so I
brought him home . . . I mean, he'd been thrown
out of a car . . . he'd have been run over . . . or
attacked by a dog if I'd left him . . .'

'Well that explains it,' Mrs James laughed,
scooping the kitten up and tickling its ears. 'As
Emily says, people can be so cruel bringing pets
into the house at Christmas and then deciding
they don't want them after all . . .'

Emily looked at her mother pleadingly. 'I had

to keep the shed door locked in case you let him out, Mum. I was waiting for the right moment to tell you . . . I thought perhaps if I could house-train him first . . .'

'No, Emily,' said Mrs Martin firmly. 'I'm very glad you rescued the kitten, but house-trained or unhouse-trained, it can't stay here. Not with Denise's allergies and Nipper.'

'But, Mum . . .'

Behind them Mrs James cleared her throat. 'I think I might have an answer to your problem. My sister is coming to stay for a couple of days next week – that's why we're painting the bathroom. I daresay she'd be quite willing to take this little fellow back to her farm. In the meantime he can curl up in a box beside our boiler . . .'

Five minutes later one very relieved Brownie climbed into the back seat of her Guider's car, a bedspread over one arm and a cat basket under the other. Truly, Emily thought, if there was ever a competition to find the world's best Guider, then Mrs James would win it hands down.

'There's just one thing,' she leant forward so that her mouth was level with the driver's ear. 'Could you remember to tell your sister the kitten already has a name? I don't want her calling him Marmalade or Ginger. I'd like her to call him *Jamie*. After you.'

Emily and the Thinking Day Fund

Emily and Sue had started to learn the recorder. Sue was very keen.

'Let's learn some duets,' she said to her friend on their way to Brownies. 'We can practise after school tomorrow.'

Emily pulled a face. 'All the duets in our recorder book are Christmas carols. We'd sound pretty silly playing *Silent Night* in February.'

Sue sighed. She really wanted to learn a duet even if it was the wrong season. But before she could think how to persuade Emily, they had reached the Brownie hall.

The meeting was about to begin. Quickly they joined the rest of the Pack in the Brownie Ring.

'Thinking Day is just two weeks away, Brownies,' Mrs James announced. 'So now is the time to be saving your pennies for the Thinking Day Fund.'

Emily wanted to give some money to the Fund but her piggy bank was empty.

'Mine too,' said Sue. 'Nobody has money in February.'

Emily was thoughtful for most of the meeting. Then, as she was putting her coat on, she stopped still and beamed. 'Your talking about duets has given me an idea for raising money,' she told Sue. 'I'll be round at your house tomorrow afternoon with my recorder.'

'Great!' said Sue. She was so pleased at the thought of playing duets with Emily, she didn't bother to ask about the rest of the idea. Emily was always having ideas, after all, and Sue was used to going along with them.

Their practice session began at four o'clock in Sue's living room. Sue's great-granny was staying for a fortnight, so she was in the room too, sitting in an armchair.

'It's a good job your great-granny's deaf,' Emily whispered to Sue after the first ten minutes. 'If we can't play better than this, my idea will never work. We sound like hens being strangled.'

'What *is* your idea?' Sue asked eagerly, but Emily wouldn't tell her.

'I won't say till I know we're going to be good enough to do it. Otherwise you'd be disappointed.'

They continued to practise, to Granny Wallace's delight, for the rest of the week, and slowly but surely their performance improved. By Friday they could manage three carols in two parts without a single wrong note. 'We're good enough for anything now,' Sue cried triumphantly. 'Go on, Emily. You've *got* to tell me your idea.'

'Not yet.' Emily enjoyed keeping her friend in suspense. 'Meet me outside the park gates at three o'clock tomorrow. Wear your Brownie uniform and bring your recorder. I'll tell you then.'

The following day Sue leaned against the park railings and watched Emily race towards her, noting the large piece of cardboard under one arm and the music stand under the other. What were they for?

'Sorry. Have you been waiting long?' Emily panted. Then, before Sue's astonished eyes, she unfolded the music stand and tossed her Brownie baseball cap down in front of it. Sue's eyes grew rounder than ever as she read what was written on the sign.

'BEAT THE CHRISTMAS RUSH. HELP BROWNIES TODAY!'

'I put in the bit about Christmas so the carols wouldn't sound funny,' Emily explained, opening their recorder book at the duet page. 'Now, we're ready to begin.'

'Begin!' squeaked Sue. 'Begin what?'

'Busking, of course. That's what they call it when musicians play in the street and people give them money. With any luck by the end of the afternoon that cap will be full. Come on.' She raised her recorder to her lips. 'Let's kick off with *Away in a manger*. After three. One . . . two . . .'

'I must be crazy,' Sue told herself as she blew. But to her amazement halfway through the second verse a lady in a headscarf threw a coin into the cap. Then an elderly couple stopped to throw something in too. The idea was working. As they started into *Silent Night*, Sue could almost see Emily's head swelling with success. And then – disaster!

'Just *what* is the meaning of this?' a voice cried sternly.

The girls glanced up. Oh dear! Their smiles faded. It was Mrs James looming before them like a thunder cloud.

'Pack up your things this minute and come along with me.'

'But . . . but . . . Mrs James . . . we're collecting for the Thinking Day Fund . . .' Emily stammered.

The frown on their Guider's face softened. There might even have been a hint of a smile at the corner of her lips. 'Well, I'm relieved to hear you aren't collecting money for yourselves, but

still you ought to check with me before you do anything like this in Brownie uniform.'

'We're very sorry,' Sue hung her head (even though it had been Emily's idea).

'We'll certainly ask you the next time,' Emily vowed. Then, glancing towards the cap, she added pleadingly: 'Now you do know, is it OK if we keep playing?'

Kindly but firmly Mrs James shook her head. The answer is no, I'm afraid. You're blocking the pavement.'

Fifteen minutes later the girls were back in Sue's living room. Emily was in a very bad mood.

'It isn't fair! All that practising – for nothing.'

Sue was still trying to think of a comforting reply when her mum and great-granny came into the room. In all that excitement she had forgotten that today was the day Granny Wallace was going home.

'Well goodbye, my dears,' the elderly lady gave them both a hug. Then she opened her handbag and took out a five pound note. 'A little something for your Brownie Fund.' She pressed it into her great granddaughter's hand. 'I have so enjoyed watching you with your whistles.'

'Gosh, thanks, Gran,' Sue gasped. She turned to her friend. 'You see, I *told* you it wasn't for nothing, Em.'

Five whole pounds! Emily's smile almost split her face in two. Yes, this more than made up for the nearly empty cap. Her idea might have gone wrong in the middle – but it had really worked out in the end.

Emily and the Swimming Gala

It was Saturday morning. 'I'm off to the swimming pool,' Emily announced.

'Can't you think of anywhere else to spend your time?' Her mum wiped the table. 'You'll dissolve if you aren't careful.'

'Not likely.' There was a determined look on Emily's face. 'Mrs James is going to pick four Brownies to take part in the District Swimming Gala. I want to be on the team.'

Stuffing a towel and her swimsuit into a plastic bag, Emily raced out of the house. She reached the pool on the dot of half past nine. I'll be first in the changing rooms, she thought. To her surprise two of her friends had beaten her to it; Helen had already changed into a sleek navy swimsuit with white spots and Jill sat huddled on a bench with a huge pink bath towel wrapped around her shoulders.

'How come you're here so early?' she asked Helen.

'I'm practising for the Gala.' The athletic red head swung her arms backwards and forwards to keep warm. 'Jill has a stopwatch so I brought her along to time me.'

Emily bundled her clothes into a locker. 'Oh good! She can time me too.' She pushed her hair into her swimming cap.

Now it was Helen's turn to look surprised. 'What would she want to do that for? Mrs James will only pick Brownies with their Advanced Swimmer badge to race in the Gala – that means Debbie, Joanne, Sarah and me.'

Jill shivered. 'Do you think it would be OK if I wore a jumper over my swimsuit and kept my specs on?'

'Don't be daft.' Helen held out her hand for the glasses. 'That's like asking if you can swim without getting wet. Right, Em? Hey, Emily, what's all the hurry? Wait for us!'

Emily was racing ahead into the shower room. She splashed through the footbath and padded on into the main hall. A turquoise expanse of water gleamed up at her. Usually she felt like leaping straight in at the deep end. But not today. Today it seemed to mock her. What Helen said made sense. Mrs James would only pick Brownies who had their Advanced Swimmer badge to take part in the races. No matter how hard she practised, she didn't stand a chance.

By this time Helen and Jill had come out of the changing room.

'Race you to the shallow end, Em,' Helen called.

There was a huge splash as the two girls jumped into the water. Heads down, arms and legs thrashing, they raced down the empty pool.

Helen won.

Jill peered at her watch. 'Three minutes twenty seconds,' she announced.

'A record!' cried Helen. 'You didn't do badly, either, Em. You weren't *that* far behind.'

Instead of answering, Emily took a deep breath and sank to the bottom of the pool blowing bubbles to the surface.

'That's brave,' said Jill when she came back up again. 'Aren't you afraid of getting water up your nose?'

Emily felt more cheerful. ''Course not. I can stay down for ages,' she boasted. 'It's like being a submarine. You might be able to swim faster, Helen, but I bet I can stay down longer. Tell you what, let's try it and see. Let's have a submarine race.'

'OK. Time us, would you, Jill? Ready, steady, GO!'

Jill blinked short-sightedly as her two friends

disappeared under the water. 'One . . . two . . . three . . . four . . .' she counted aloud.

On the seventy-eighth count Helen burst to the surface followed by a crimson-faced Emily on the seventy-ninth.

'What did I tell you!' she gasped.

'Submarine races aren't important. There's no such thing as a submarine race in the Swimming Gala,' shrugged Helen. She pushed out from the side and set off up the pool with strong even strokes.

Emily hauled herself on to the edge beside Jill.

'Here. You time her.' Jill handed her the stop-watch. 'I can't see the deep end properly without my specs. It's just a blur of blobs.'

'Does Helen look like a blob?' asked Emily hopefully.

'Yes,' said Jill. 'A big navy spotted one.' She stood up and walked towards the exit. 'I'm off to get changed. I'm freezing.'

A few minutes later Helen swam back to the edge.

Emily slipped into the water. It seemed the perfect opportunity to wipe the smug smile off Helen's face.

'Jill's in the changing room,' she said airily. 'Timing you was like watching a giant spotted blob, she said. It got on her nerves.'

Just as Emily had expected, Helen's smile disappeared. 'She didn't say that!'

'She did so. If anyone told me I looked like a spotted blob I wouldn't dare take part in a Swimming Gala – unless there was a submarine race where nobody could see me.'

'You shut up,' Helen's voice was husky. 'Mrs James wouldn't pick you for the Gala in a million years. And I couldn't care less what Jill says. She's nothing but a stupid scaredy cat.'

'She's good at drawing and describing things,' said Emily, and submarined down to the smooth tiled bottom of the pool.

With four feet of water above her head, Emily opened her eyes and watched Helen's legs climbing up the steps.

Part of her wanted to pop back up to the surface and shout, 'It's all right, Helen. Jill didn't really call you a giant spotted blob. It's just she can't see properly.' But another part of her wanted Helen to feel as miserable as *she* felt about not getting on to the team for the Swimming Gala. So she stayed where she was.

Helen's legs disappeared. Emily was about to come up for air when, a couple of inches from her big toe, she spotted a minute pebble-shaped piece of glass.

Gosh! That's dangerous, she thought. She

managed to hold her breath for an extra second –
just long enough to pick it up.

'Look what I found on the bottom of the pool,'
she told the pool attendant. 'Someone could have
cut their foot. It's a good thing I learnt to hold my
breath and keep my eyes open under water as
part of my Brownie Swimmer badge.'

'It is indeed,' agreed the pool attendant. 'What
did you say your name was?'

Emily told him and went on into the changing

room. Now that she wasn't likely to get a place on the Swimming Gala team, she didn't feel like practising any more.

She found Jill sitting on a bench, wrapped up in her big pink bath towel, looking as if she was about to burst into tears.

'Helen's stopped speaking to me,' she wailed. 'She was coming round to my house to play this afternoon. But now she says she doesn't want to. It's because I'm no good at swimming, isn't it, Emily? That's why she doesn't want to be my friend any more.'

Oh dear! Emily felt really mean. Jill was quiet and shy and didn't have much confidence in herself. Now she was upset – and it was all Emily's fault. There was nothing else for it. She had to tell Jill the truth.

'You mean Helen thinks I called her a giant blob,' gasped Jill. 'Emily! How could you!'

'The way she acted made me mad. I'm really sorry now. Hey wait, Jill! You can't go running outside in a bath towel!'

But Jill had gone.

Oh dear! Emily felt more miserable than ever. She couldn't swim fast enough to be in the Swimming Gala, and now she had fallen out with half the members of her Brownie Six.

The rest of the day was rotten. Helen and Jill

played together at Jill's house and they didn't call for Emily. The same thing happened on Monday. They ran off together after school and Emily was left behind. 'I don't feel like going to Brownies tonight,' she told her mum when she got home. 'I feel like staying at home and watching telly.'

'You'll do no such thing,' said Mrs Martin firmly. 'Your Guider was on the phone half an hour ago to make sure you'd be there.'

Mrs James ringing her mum! Emily was so shocked she almost choked on a fruit gum. Had Helen and Jill been telling tales? Did they want Mrs James to tick her off in front of the whole Pack?

She got into her uniform as usual after tea, but hung about in the hallway.

'My tummy's sore,' she moaned.

'Too many chips. Walking to Brownies will cure it. Off you go.'

Emily set off down the street, walking so slowly a snail could have overtaken her. Finally she reached the Brownie hall. She could see through the window that the Sixes were already in their Brownie Ring. Her heart beat faster. Mrs James was making the announcements. If she could just stay outside until they were over . . .

'Hurry up, Emily! You're keeping everyone

waiting . . .' Too late! She had been spotted. Mrs James had sent Linda out to bring her in.

'There you are at last!' she cried as Emily took her place in the Ring. 'In a moment I shall tell the Brownies what you've been up to.'

Emily went hot and cold. This was even worse than she'd expected.

'But first,' Mrs James continued, 'there is the matter of the team for the Swimming Gala. Four Brownies have passed their Advanced Swimmers badges and they will be representing us on Saturday week. Let's have a Pack Salute for Helen, Joanne, Sarah and Debbie.'

'Good luck! Good luck! Very good luck!' clapped the Brownies.

'Now,' said Mrs James in a loud voice, 'I want to tell you a little story I heard last week.'

Emily squirmed in her place.

'Last week,' the Guider went on, 'a friend of mine lost the stone from her engagement ring. She spent a whole day on her hands and knees, searching the house from top to bottom. She thought she had lost it for ever. But thanks to one of our Brownies, her story has a happy ending. A Brownie from this Pack spotted the lost diamond on the floor of the swimming pool and gave it to the pool attendant. My friend has asked me to say a special thank you to the Brownie concerned, and to present her with a small reward. So let's see how loudly we can cheer for – EMILY MARTIN.'

Well, who would have believed it? The piece of glass had been a valuable diamond! Emily felt like rushing round hugging every Brownie in sight. But first she had to put things right with Helen and Jill.

'I'm really sorry for what I said,' she told them. 'You deserved your place on the team, Helen. I'll be at the Gala, cheering you on!'

Helen grinned. 'I'm sorry too, Em. I shouldn't have said that submarine races weren't important. Looks like they can come in handy, doesn't it Jill?'

Jill sighed. 'I suppose so,' she muttered.

Emily winked at Helen. She knew what was wrong.

'Never mind, Jill. You'll soon be able to swim,' she said. 'My reward for finding the diamond is ten swimming lessons and I'm giving them to you.'

'To me!' gasped Jill. 'Swimming lessons! That's fantastic!'

Helen winked back. 'I wonder what sort of a blob her instructor will be?'

Emily and the Missing Gnomes

Every morning on her way to school Emily counted things. She counted weeds as she walked down her front path. She counted pigeons as she passed the park. And finally, just before she turned into the school playground, she counted Ma Green's gnomes.

Ma Green was the school caretaker and lived in the cottage beside the school gates. She had filled the little garden with an army of coloured gnomes.

Now it was the holidays and Ma Green had gone to stay with her sister in Blackpool. Emily was sure that she would bring back another gnome to add to her collection.

'That will make twenty-four altogether,' she told Sue, as the two friends sat on the school wall.

'Twenty-one,' Sue corrected her. 'She has twenty now. I've just counted.'

'Well you've counted wrong,' said Emily. 'She

has twenty-three. I should know. I'm the one who counts them usually.'

'So count them again.'

Emily did. 'Seventeen, eighteen, nineteen, twenty,' she finished with a frown. 'That's funny.'

'Maybe you made a mistake,' said Sue.

Emily was certain she hadn't. Three gnomes had gone missing.

Puzzling over the mystery kept her awake that night. She worried about what would happen when Ma Green got home.

First thing next morning she was back at the cottage to see if the gnomes had come back. Carefully she counted: 'Fifteen, sixteen, seventeen, eighteen.' Eighteen! Oh no! That *couldn't* be right. But it was. She sat down on the wall, shaking her head. Two more missing. Things were going from bad to worse.

Emily spent the next six hours behind a gooseberry bush. She went home for lunch, of course — otherwise her mum would have worried. But she was back in position without even waiting for pudding. It was a very boring way to spend a whole day of the school holidays. But something had to be done. Ma Green was such a friendly caretaker. The last thing Emily wanted was for her to walk into a gnomeless garden.

And then at five o'clock, just as she was about

to crawl from her hiding place for tea, it happened. Two more gnomes disappeared. And Emily was there to see how they went. They were being stolen. A man had slipped into the garden and walked out with a gnome-filled plastic bag under each arm. But the really amazing thing was that she had recognised the thief. It was Mr Brocklehurst, her headmaster.

'What would you do if you saw someone stealing things?' Emily asked her mum at the tea-table.

Mrs Martin thought for a moment. 'That would depend. What things are we talking about?'

'School things – sort of.'

'Ah, then I would report it to the Headmaster,' said Emily's mum.

Emily sighed. If only it could be so simple. 'You mean, you wouldn't go straight to the police?'

'Not to begin with, it would be better to let the Headmaster or some other adult decide what to do.' She paused and looked at her daughter. 'Did someone you know take something, dear? Was it one of your friends?'

'Um . . . oh no . . . nothing like that.' Emily gulped her orange. She didn't think it would be fair to land the problem on her mum. After all, she had dishes to wash and clothes to iron and Sophie to put to bed. She would never have time to go and report Mr Brocklehurst to the police. Still, telling another adult sounded like a good idea.

Half an hour later she knocked on Mrs James's door.

'Why hello, Emily!' The Guider didn't seem in the least put out to find a serious-faced Brownie on her doorstep. 'What can I do for you?'

'It's a bit tricky really,' said Emily. 'I've discovered someone is a thief.'

'In that case . . .' Mrs James took her by the shoulder and steered her into the house. 'You'd better tell me the whole story . . .'

'Mr Brocklehurst!' she exclaimed when Emily had finished her tale. 'Mr Brocklehurst! I don't believe it!'

This was exactly what Emily had been afraid of. 'But it's true. I saw him. He put the gnomes in bags and off he went. Please, Mrs James, you've got to go to the police. Ma Green won't have a single gnome left otherwise.'

'Leave it to me.' The Guider nodded wisely. 'I'll sort things out and be in touch in the morning.'

For the second night in a row Emily didn't sleep well. She had a nightmare. She couldn't remember it very clearly next morning but it had something to do with Mr Brocklehurst stuffing

Mrs James into a plastic bag full of gooseberries.

Shortly after breakfast the telephone rang and Emily ran to answer it.

'Emily Martin? This is Mr Brocklehurst's secretary speaking. The Headmaster wants you to come to his office this morning. At ten o'clock, please.'

Emily was shaking in her shoes. It's like being told to take a dip with a crocodile she thought as she turned into the school gates. To her surprise the first person she saw was Mrs James.

'Good girl. Bang on time,' smiled the Guider. 'Now come along. Mr Brocklehurst has something to show you.'

To her even greater surprise, Mr Brocklehurst was smiling when he opened the office door.

'Ah, our keen-eyed Brownie,' he boomed. 'Follow me.'

Emily followed – round the corner – up a flight of stairs – and into the art room.

'Now then.' The Headmaster flung open the art-store door.

A wonderful sight met Emily's eyes. Seven gleaming gnomes, freshly painted in all the colours of the rainbow.

'My holiday hobby,' Mr Brocklehurst explained. 'I wanted to smarten up as many as possible before Mrs Green's return. I was hoping

to keep my efforts secret . . . but . . . well . . . this young lady proved too observant.'

'Brownies learn to be Wide Awake,' Mrs James nodded.

Well, what a relief! Her headmaster wasn't a thief after all. 'Don't worry, Mr Brocklehurst,' Emily beamed. 'Brownies learn to keep secrets too.'

A Pen Pal for Emily

Emily jumped out of bed, looked at the clock, pulled off her pyjamas, pulled on her clothes, then held her breath, looked at the clock again and cheered, 'Twenty-eight seconds, that's a record!'

She always challenged herself to dress quickly on Saturday mornings and this Saturday she was in the biggest ever hurry to get downstairs. She was expecting a letter – a pale blue airmail envelope with an American stamp. Her first letter from her new pen pal.

It was almost a month now since the post box secretary at Girl Guide Headquarters had given her Darling's name and address.

'Her name is *Darlene*, not Darling!' her mum had said.

Emily had been too excited to listen.

She had written that very evening; two full pages, telling Darling all about herself – about being a Brownie and working for her Road badge.

About having a dog called Nipper and a best friend called Sue and a sister called Sophie.

'Write back soon,' she had finished, 'and tell me what the weather is like in America and if you have a dog.'

Today she was sure there would be a reply.

She raced downstairs into the living room and peered out of the window. No sign of the postman. She shut her eyes and began to count. Counting to one hundred would make him arrive sooner she thought.

'Ninety-eight, ninety-nine, one hundred!' she counted. The doorbell rang but it wasn't the postman. It was Sue, her round freckled face pink with delight.

'Guess what Emily!' Her eyes were popping with excitement, 'I got another letter from my pen pal this morning. Pages and pages. She told me all about Brownies and guess what? The things she does sound the same as the things we do, only the names are different. Like being a Ready Helper for them is the same as Lending a Hand for us. Look, I've brought the letter round to show you . . .'

Suddenly she noticed Emily's face and stopped.

'What's up? Haven't you heard from your pen pal yet?'

Emily shook her head glumly, biting her lip.

She knew now that the postman had come early and driven straight past her house. It wasn't fair! Sue had had two letters and she hadn't even had one.

'Let's forget all about pen pals, Sue,' she said crossly. 'If you ask me Darling probably doesn't know how to write.'

'You could always ask for another name and address,' said Sue.

Emily sighed, 'That probably wouldn't be any good. Probably the new one wouldn't write either and I'd have to get another address and write another letter and another and another. I'd rather just forget it, OK?'

'OK,' nodded Sue and followed her into the living room. She felt sorry. She had been hoping that they could work together for their Brownie Friendship badge but there wasn't much chance of that now. Not after the way Darlene had let Emily down. She pocketed her own letter with a thoughtful frown. Then smiled to herself.

She had had an idea.

Two more weeks went by and the postman posted something through Emily's letter box nearly every day. There were bills, letters for her parents and a postcard but there was no sign of a letter from Darling.

By the end of two weeks Emily had given up hope.

Sue came round to play that Saturday as usual, arriving on the doorstep first thing after breakfast with a *Brownie Badge Book* in a brown paper bag.

'What did you bring that for?' asked Emily.

'To find out what I need to do for my Brownie Friendship badge,' said Sue. 'Having a pen pal in California has made me want to work for it.'

Emily felt cross and hurt inside, the way she always did when something reminded her that her pen pal didn't write.

'You're not going to work for it here, are you?' she said sulkily. 'I mean, I got the operation game out. I thought we were going to play that! I mean, if you want to work for your Brownie Friendship badge and not play operations you should have stayed at home.'

The trouble with Sue was that she was a very difficult person to fight with. Now she didn't even notice Emily's sulks. She just smiled and cocked her head to one side, like a plump, bright-eyed robin with a secret.

'I've got a surprise for you in my pocket, Emily,' she said. 'I'll give you three guesses what it is.'

'A packet of fruit gums,' said Emily hopefully.

Fruit gums were her favourite sweets – because they lasted.

Sue shook her head. 'Better than that.'

'Two packets of fruit gums?' said Emily.

'Wrong again!' said Sue. 'Go on. Think! It's something you've been waiting for for ages.'

The only thing Emily could think of was a pony.

'It's in my pocket!' laughed Sue. 'Don't be dopey.'

'Give up,' said Emily, 'what is it?'

Sue put her hand in her pocket and pulled out . . . a pale blue airmail envelope with an American stamp.

Emily stared. She could hardly believe her eyes. *Miss Emily Martin, c/o Miss Susan King.* Yes, that was what it said.

'Well, aren't you going to open it?' demanded Sue.

Eagerly Emily took the envelope, slit it across the top, then carefully smoothed the thin blue sheet out on the table.

'Dear Emily,' she read, 'my name is Darrel-Ann. I am nine years old. I hope you will be my pen pal because you sound real neat.'

'Neat means nice,' Sue chirped. 'My pen pal Laura is always saying that. Darrel-Ann is her best friend.'

'But how did she find out about me?'

'I wrote and told her. You don't mind, do you?'

'Hey listen, this is fantastic! She wants to be a vet!'

'Well, you wanted a pen pal who likes animals, didn't you?' asked Sue.

Emily was too taken up with her letter to answer.

Emily Finds Out About Ballet

Emily raced home from Brownies, singing the new song she had learnt in Pow Wow at the top of her voice.

Everything was wonderful. Helen's mum had invited her for tea on Wednesday. She would ask if it was all right the minute she got in through the door.

She raced round the corner. 'Oh bother!' Suddenly she didn't feel like singing any more.

Outside the front gate of her house stood a familiar red car.

She walked on slowly, remembering something her mum had said: 'You can pick your friends, Emily, but not your relatives.'

It was such a pity, she thought. If she'd been given the chance to pick a relative, she would never in a million years have chosen Auntie Ann.

Auntie Ann was her mum's older sister. Being older, Auntie Ann thought she knew best; better than Emily's teacher, better than Emily's mum, better than Emily's Brownie *Handbook*.

Slowly Emily walked up the path trying to work out who she would have picked as an aunt if anyone had bothered to ask her beforehand – Mrs James, perhaps? Or the lady on *Blue Peter*? Oops! She tripped over the doorstep, fell against a plant stand and sent three cacti and a spider plant crashing to the ground.

This meant that she was on all fours scooping compost back into pots when her mum and Auntie Ann came out of the kitchen.

'What did I tell you, Margaret?' Auntie Ann wore her usual I-know-best expression. 'The child is clumsy. We must do something about it. Emily, my dear, your mother has something to tell you.'

'Have you, Mum?' pouted Emily, suspecting trouble.

Mrs Martin knelt down. 'Your aunt has very kindly arranged for you to go to ballet lessons with cousin Denise on Wednesdays,' she said.

'From half past three until a quarter past four. I'll pick you up after school,' pronounced Auntie Ann.

A *ballet* lesson! On *Wednesday*!

'But, Mum, I've been invited to Helen's,' Emily wailed.

'I'm sure you can play with your little friend

another time,' snapped her aunt. 'Going to balle[t]
is much more important.'

'I would like you to try it, Emily. For a few
weeks anyway.'

Emily glared at her mum across the mess o[f]
leaves. It wasn't fair. She wanted to go to Helen's[,]
not to some stupid ballet class. Ballet was fo[r]
sissies.

'Please, Emily,' said Mrs Martin.

She looked worried, the way she often did when
Auntie Ann filled the house with knowing-better
ideas. Perhaps I should make it a sort of Browni[e]
Good Turn, Emily thought suddenly. After all[,]
I'm lucky to have such a nice mum. Another mum
might not have said please – especially not afte[r]
me wrecking her plant stand.

'Oh all *right*,' she sighed. 'If *you* want me to, I'l[l]
go.'

In school the next day she looked for Helen a[t]
lunch time to break the bad news. She searche[d]
the playground, the classrooms, and the toilets[,]
but Helen was nowhere to be found. In the en[d]
Emily stopped looking and sat down on a wall[.]
She was puzzled. She had seen her friend going
into class that morning which meant she couldn'[t]
be sick. So what had happened to her? What i[f]
she'd been *kidnapped*?

As this horrible thought crossed Emily's mind, who should plonk himself down on the wall but Helen's brother Henry.

Henry was two years older than Helen, three years older than Emily, and could jump higher and longer than any other boy in the school. Helen had even called her pony after him – in Emily's eyes the greatest compliment a brother could ever be paid – because she hoped the pony would turn out to be a good jumper too.

'Henry,' blurted Emily, before she could stop herself. 'Helen's disappeared. I'm afraid she's been kidnapped.'

He took one look at her small solemn face and then threw his head back and roared with laughter. 'No such luck! She's at the dentist,' he gasped. 'She told me to ask you if Wednesday was all right.'

Emily felt as if she had shrunk to the size of a tiny black beetle and wanted to disappear into a crack in the wall. Henry was laughing at her. He thought she was silly. Telling him about the ballet class now would be unbearable.

She hung her head and muttered as quickly as she could, 'I can't come on Wednesday, I've got a class.'

'I've a class on Wednesdays too,' Henry had stopped laughing, and sounded interested. 'What's yours?'

She took a deep breath, looked him straight in the eyes and said: 'Judo.'

Before he could ask any more questions, she hopped to the ground.

'Goodbye then.'

'You'll have to tell me more about that the next time you're round,' he grinned.

She ran away without answering, afraid she would burst into tears. Did he suspect the truth? It wasn't fair. Why had she ever thought of going to ballet as a Brownie Good Turn? Now she would never be able to visit Helen's pony again.

On Wednesday afternoon, at half past three on the dot, Auntie Ann's car drew up outside the school.

Emily trailed out of the playground and climbed into the back seat beside Denise.

Her aunt smiled into the driving-mirror without turning round. 'Hello Emily. Looking forward to our first ballet lesson, are we?'

'Not a lot,' said Emily gloomily.

The ballet classes were held in the town hall next door to the library – a new modern building with windows right down to the floor. As soon as they arrived, Emily pulled up the hood of her anorak, jumped out of the car and made a dash for it, terrified that one of Henry's friends – or worse

70

till, Henry himself – would look up from a book
and spot her.

A few minutes later Auntie Ann followed her
into the hall.

'I've two new students for you here. Emily, as
you can see, is very eager and Denise is very shy,'
he told the teacher. 'Say good afternoon to Miss
Old, girls.'

Despite her name, Miss Old was young and
wore a sweatshirt with London College of Dance
and Drama printed on the front. 'I'm delighted to
hear you're so keen, Emily. Now just go over to
the bench and get changed,' she said, her blue
eyes twinkling.

Auntie Ann had brought two pairs of white
tights, two white T-shirts, two white hairbands
and two pairs of pink ballet shoes in a plastic bag.
Emily pulled on her tights and T-shirt and allowed all her hair to be scraped back from her
face into a tiny pony-tail at the back of her head.
As she put on her shoes she felt a faint stir of
excitement. She had caught sight of herself in a
long mirror. She looked totally different. She
wasn't Emily Martin any more. She was a
dancer.

'Come along, girls,' said Miss Old. Emily took
Denise by the hand, because her cousin was
much too shy to 'come along' on her own, and

followed the rest of the class into the main hall.

The other girls had been learning ballet for at least a month and knew what they were doing. As soon as Miss Old said 'first position' they all stuck out their feet and curved their arms out from their sides. Emily didn't wait to be told. She simply copied them. And Denise copied her.

'Keep those seats in, girls,' called Miss Old.

So the lesson went on, with Emily copying the other girls and Denise copying Emily and Miss Old calling things about arms and toes and seats. Then came the exciting bit. Miss Old announced that they were going to practise a dance for the show.

'I want you to pretend to be flowers,' she said. 'Lots of different coloured flowers, growing in a wood.'

She asked the lady at the piano to play some flower music.

Tinkle, tinkle, tinkle, went the flower music. Emily looked around and saw the other girls curled up on the ground, growing gracefully. She pictured the most magnificent blossom in her Auntie Ann's porch and started growing too, shooting out buds and leaves and opening petals as effortlessly as if she'd spent the first eight years of life in a pot.

'Well done, girls,' called Miss Old, when

everyone was in full bloom. 'Emily, can you tell me what sort of flower you are?'

'A prize-winning geranium,' said Emily proudly.

'Excellent. Exactly what we need to brighten up our wood.' Miss Old's eyes twinkled more than ever. 'Just remember to point those toes.'

Now Emily had a problem. She really really wanted to be a prize-winning geranium in Miss Old's show, but she was really really worried in case Helen's brother Henry found out.

With any luck he wouldn't recognise her in her ballet costume, she thought as she followed the other girls out of the hall to get changed.

The next class was already lined up and waiting to go in.

'Oh look, Emily!' Denise giggled and pointed at a group of boys in black tights.

Boys? Doing ballet? Emily stared. Then gasped. Oh no! She knew one of them. She would have to get out fast.

'Someone's in a hurry! Well, this is a surprise! It's Emily Martin.' Helen's brother Henry caught her by the arm.

'Let go of me . . . you great . . . big . . . bully . . .'

He grinned down at her. 'You're meant to be at judo.'

She flushed as red as a fire-engine. 'If . . . if . . .

you call me a sissy, I . . . I'll . . . ladder your tights.'

'Now why should I do that?' Henry let go of her arm, flexing his muscles. 'Ballet isn't for sissies. Dancers have to be really athletic and tough.'

He wasn't laughing. What a relief! 'I'm going to be a really tough geranium in the show,' beamed Emily. 'What sort of a flower are you?'

'No sort,' said Henry. 'I'm the wind. I have to

spin and leap about the stage, and knock the flowers down flat.'

Emily lifted her chin. He would have a hard job flattening her! She could hardly wait until next week to see him try.

'Well, girls, how did you get on?' was her aunt's first question when she and Denise climbed into the car.

It was only then that Emily remembered she wasn't supposed to enjoy ballet; that she'd only agreed to go to the class as a Brownie Good Turn for her mum; that she certainly shouldn't be looking forward to next week.

'It was OK, I suppose,' she growled. But she was beaming. She couldn't help it. Nor could she help thinking, as the car pulled to a halt outside her house, that every now and again – perhaps once or twice in a million years – Auntie Ann *might* know best after all.

The Pony Plan

'Can I have my pocket money, please?' said Emily.

Her mum opened her purse and took out a fifty pence piece. 'I'm about to take Sophie for a walk to the shop. Why not come with us and spend it?' she said.

'No, thanks.' Emily shook her head firmly. 'I'm saving up.'

A little later, when her mum and Sophie had gone, she fetched her Bruno Bear money box, pulled off the bear's head and emptied his tummy on to the kitchen table. Out came twelve twenty pence coins, six fifty pence coins, five one pound coins and a clatter of pennies.

'Over ten pounds!' she counted. 'Brilliant! That's bound to be enough.'

She screwed Bruno back together again and went out into the garden shed.

What a mess! For the last three years her dad had been planning to put up shelves, but he still hadn't got round to it. Everything was sitting on the ground – jam jars, plant pots, paint tins, cardboard boxes.

Emily set to work. For the next three quarters of an hour she tidied jam jars into plant pots, plant pots into paint tins and paint tins into cardboard boxes. Then she moved the boxes to a side of the shed leaving a nice clear square in the middle of the floor. She brushed all the spiders she could catch out into the garden and went back into the house again.

Her mum was in the kitchen unpacking groceries.

'My goodness!' she said. 'Have you been having a picnic in the chimney?'

'I've been tidying the garden shed,' Emily told her.

Mrs Martin almost dropped her eggs in surprise. 'What's got into you? That's the first time you've ever tidied anything without being asked. Is this some special Brownie Challenge?'

Emily beamed. 'I can't tell you what it is right now. You'll have to wait till I come home from Helen's to find out.'

'Well, you can't go to Helen's looking like that. Go straight upstairs and have a bath.'

Emily sang to herself as she lay soaking in bubbles. She had been planning this for weeks, ever since her granny had given her five pounds for her birthday. That was when she had the idea of saving up for a pony of her own and keeping it in the garden shed. She had over ten pounds now and the shed had been made into a stable. There was only one thing that might stop her bringing a pony home that afternoon. She didn't know where to buy one, but Helen would know. Helen knew all about ponies. Singing more loudly than ever Emily swooshed the water up the sides of the bath. How surprised everyone would be to see her galloping across the park to her house!

'It might take me a while to get home, Mum,' she said when it was nearly time for Helen's mum to collect her. 'I won't be coming back by car.'

Her mum thought she was joking, 'How are you coming back then? By tractor?' she teased.

'By pony,' Emily almost said.

But just at that moment Helen and Mrs Hamilton arrived at the door.

'What do you want to do?' asked Helen as soon as Emily got out of the car.

Emily looked around. 'What I would really like to do,' she thought, 'is to swop places with Helen and live on a farm with dogs and cats and hens and cows and a pony!'

'I'd like to see Henry,' she said out loud.

'Four-legged Henry or two-legged Henry?' Helen grinned.

Emily got the joke, 'Four-legged Henry, of course.'

Imagine having a pony and a brother with the same name, she marvelled as they strolled down the lane to the paddock. The last thing she would want was a pony called Sophie!

They reached the paddock gate, and there was Henry grazing on the other side of the field, his smooth golden coat gleaming in the sun. As soon as Helen called, he lifted his head, and with a flick of his creamy tail, came trotting over to them. He was smashing, Emily thought. She hoped her pony would look exactly the same.

'Here, give him these,' Helen filled her hand with things that looked like small brown beans.

'Pony nuts,' she explained.

Emily held her hand out flat, thrilling at the velvet feel of Henry's lips as they brushed the pony nuts into his mouth.

Then she had a horrible thought. What would her pony eat when she brought him home? There was only a small patch of grass in her garden.

'Helen,' she said in a small voice, 'would it cost more than fifty pence a week to feed a pony? If you didn't have a field, I mean.'

'I'll say it would,' said Helen cheerfully. 'Dad says keeping Henry costs a fortune!'

Emily's heart sank right down into her shoes. She definitely couldn't spend more than fifty pence a week on her pony. She felt so miserable, she stopped patting Henry's nose. He pushed his head against her hand, but she moved away.

'What's wrong?' asked Helen.

'N-nothing.'

'Then why are you crying?'

'I'm not crying. The wind is making my eyes water, that's all.'

'You're afraid of Henry? Is that it?' persisted Helen.

'Don't be silly. I love him – your pony, I mean, not your brother. It's just that I had this brilliant plan but it's all gone wrong.'

'Let's hear it,' said Helen.

Four hours later, Emily hopped out of Helen's mum's car and tore down the path to the front door.

'Thanks a million, Mrs Hamilton! Thanks a million, Helen!' she yelled.

Then, beaming from ear to ear, she let herself in.

'Yoohoo, Mum!' she called. 'I'm back, guess what! I want to spend all my birthday money on something really special, but Mrs Hamilton said I was to ask you first.'

'Well, what is it?'

'A pair of jodhpurs and a jacket and a riding hat. They belong to Helen, only they are too small. Helen said I could have them for ten pounds and go out every week and learn to ride Henry. Well, Mum, what do you say? Is it all right? Go on. Say yes. Please.'

Mrs Martin smiled. 'Yes, Emily,' she said.

Emily Lets Her Hair Down

A small plump figure ran into the girls' cloakroom and looked around her. Ah! At last! She spotted a pair of feet poking out beneath the pile of coats behind the door.

'Emily, is that you?' cried Sue. 'I've been hunting everywhere. The Brownie meeting's about to begin.'

'Shhh. Keep your voice down,' came the muffled reply. 'I'm hiding.'

'Hiding?' Sue took two steps backwards and sat on a bench. 'What for?'

'So the other Brownies won't laugh at me. Auntie Ann did my hair before I came out and she's turned me into a freak.'

'You poor thing!' Sue shook her head. For the last three days – ever since Emily's mum had gone to spend a few days on board her dad's ship – she had felt truly sorry for her friend; Emily had been forced to stay with her least favourite relative – the dreaded Auntie Ann. 'Never mind.

84

Come out and show me,' she encouraged. 'It mightn't be as bad as you think.'

But it was.

'Oh dear!' Sue started to giggle. Auntie Ann had twisted Emily's fair hair in two tight little plaits, each finished off with a neat yellow bow. They stuck out, almost horizontally, on either side of her head.

'You'd think my ears were on a skewer!' Emily groaned into the mirror. 'It took her nearly half an hour. She went on and on about what an improvement it was and how much neater and tidier I looked and how she would show Mum exactly how to do it when she got back . . . Oh Sue! What am I going to do? I can't stand in the Brownie Ring like something about to be barbecued.'

At this, Sue lifted the end of one of her own long brown braids and twirled it under her friend's nose. 'I can plait hair pretty well . . .'

'Hang on!' Emily beamed. 'You mean if I brushed my hair out, you'd fix it back this way after the meeting and Auntie Ann would never notice a thing . . .'

'Well . . . um . . .' Sue hesitated.

'Brilliant! Why didn't I think of that sooner?' Emily grabbed her two stumpy little tails. Yank. Yank. She pulled off the ribbons. 'Hurrah!

Goodbye plaits!' she cheered. 'Quick, Sue! Lend me a comb.'

Mrs James had already announced the first Brownie activity of the evening by the time the two girls arrived in the hall. 'We're making greetings cards,' she explained, handing Emily and Sue two thick sheets of folded paper.

'They can be birthday cards or get well cards, or thank-you cards – whatever you like,' she went on. 'But don't just use crayons and felt tips to draw pictures on the front. Go outside. Look round the grounds and see what interesting things you can find – leaves perhaps, or milk bottle tops – and glue them on to make your designs.'

Forgetting all about Auntie Ann, Emily raced off. 'It's like three challenges rolled into one,' she told Sue happily. 'We're making something, we're having fun out-of-doors and we have to be wide awake to find something really unusual to stick on our cards.'

'Look, Emily. What's that?' Sue spotted an unusual splash of colour deep in the hedge beside the playground. She knelt down. Avoiding the brambles she reached in between the leaves, and came out with a crumpled piece of bright red tissue paper.

'It isn't even torn or dirty,' Emily breathed as they smoothed the paper out on the ground. 'How

87

about cutting it up into flower shapes and using little bits of grass for the stems?'

Eagerly they set to work. Emily cut out the shapes, and Sue glued them into place – making a bouquet of six red flowers on the front of her friend's card and six on her own.

'You couldn't buy anything as nice in a shop,' Sue pronounced, standing back to admire the general effect. 'I'm going to send mine to my cousin Jason. He'll be thirteen on Wednesday. What'll you do with yours?'

'Um . . .' Emily scratched her head. This was a problem. None of her relations had birthdays that week. None of them were sick either. And as for saying thank you . . . well, she supposed there was one person she could thank. She frowned. It seemed so stupid – to thank someone for doing all sorts of bossy interfering things. Still – she looked again at the card – it seemed even stupider to waste it.

Slowly she lifted a brown felt tip.

'To Auntie Ann. Thank you for looking after me,' she wrote inside.

Just then Jill came over to see how they were getting on.

'Hey. Your cards have turned out really well,' she eyed their efforts critically, her head on one side. 'Do you want to see mine?'

'Yes please,' Emily and Sue chimed.

'Da . . . da . . . da . . . dum . . .' From inside her Brownie Handbook Jill produced her creation. Get well soon. She had printed the words above an impressive bowl of silky yellow fruit – one melon, two grapefruit and a bunch of bananas.

'Lovely!' Sue beamed.

But somehow Emily couldn't seem to work up much enthusiasm.

'Um . . . what did you make the fruit out of?' she asked in a small, anxious voice.

If she was looking worried before Jill spoke, she looked absolutely panic-stricken when she heard her reply.

'Hair ribbons,' Jill announced happily. 'Two old hair ribbons I found lying on the bench in the girls' cloakroom.'

Emily clapped her hand to her mouth. 'Oh Sue! What'll we do now! Auntie Ann's going to *kill* me,' she groaned.

All the way back to her aunt's house, sitting beside Sue in the rear of the car, she rehearsed her excuses.

'You'll never guess what, Auntie Ann. Just as I was going into the Brownie hall there was this really strong whirlwind and – whoosh – it blew the ribbons and elastic bands straight off my hair.'

Or, 'You're not going to believe this, Auntie Ann. You know those yellow ribbons you tied on my plaits? Well, there must have been a fault in them. Because halfway through the Brownie meeting they just sort of fell apart . . .'

'Good luck, Em,' Sue squeezed her hand sympathetically as the car pulled up at the house.

Slowly, ever so slowly, Emily trailed in through the front door. Outside the living room she paused for a moment, taking one last long trembling breath. She knew her excuses wouldn't work. 'I'm sorry.' That was all she could say.

And then she heard the voices. Happy excited voices. One male. One female. Her face lit up. She flung open the door. And yes!

'Mum! Dad! What are *you* doing here?'

'Surprise! Surprise!' her father swept her off her feet into his arms. 'The ship's docked for refurbishing. We got the first available flight when we heard – and Ann was good enough to pick us up at the airport . . .'

'You mean . . . I can come home with you . . . *this minute*?'

'That's the general idea. Any objections?'

'Of course not.' For the sake of good manners, Emily managed not to explode with delight.

But she still had to make her apology. Even as

she clasped her hands together and jumped for joy, she imagined Auntie Ann's eyes boring into the back of her plaitless head. Bravely, she turned round. 'I'm sorry about my hair. It's just . . . the plaits didn't . . .'

It was only then she realised she'd spoken too soon. Her aunt wasn't listening. She was opening the card Emily had thrown down on the coffee table. She was studying the words Emily had

written inside. She was actually smiling!

'Yes . . . well . . . I don't expect to be appreciated but it *is* nice when . . . I mean . . .' She positioned the card on the mantelpiece as carefully as if it had been bone china. 'I really do *try*.'

Emily could hardly believe her ears. Auntie Ann – almost in tears – over a hand-made thank-you card! She felt a sudden rush of sympathy. It was true: her aunt *did* try. She spent all day, every day, trying to knock things into shape, the house, the garden, her niece's hair.

Now her stay had come to an end, Emily could afford to be generous. She flung her arms round the tall woman's bony waist, squeezing as she spoke.

'I made the card specially and I meant every word. No girl could ever ask for a more trying auntie than you.'

Emily Knows What To Do

Helen's mum popped her head into the living room. 'I'm just nipping in next door. You'll be all right on your own for a few minutes, won't you?'

'We'll be fine, Mum.' Helen smiled across at Emily. 'As soon as the rain stops we're going outside to see the pony. It hasn't stopped yet, has it?'

'I'm afraid not. Well, behave yourselves, girls, and Henry,' Mrs Smith raised her voice, 'no TV until you've finished your homework, understand?'

On the other side of the living room, Helen's spiky-haired older brother glanced up from his arithmetic. 'No, Mum. I mean – yes, Mum . . .'

'See you soon then.' The front door banged shut.

Henry immediately leant back in his chair and plonked his Doc Martens on the table. 'She's gone. Quick! Turn on the box.'

'Naughty! Naughty!' His sister waggled her

finger at him. 'No teevie-weevie for Henry-wenry till he's finished his sumsie-wumsies.'

Henry shifted his boots back down again. 'It wasn't *me* I was thinking about,' he said crossly. 'It was Emily, stuck in here with nothing to do and no one to talk to except a prune like *you*.'

'Helen isn't a prune,' declared Emily loyally. 'And we're not doing nothing. We're discussing Brownie badges.'

'Stupid Brownie badges.' Henry took aim with his pencil case and knocked the *Brownie Badge Book* off the table.

'Bulls-eye!' he cheered. 'I got a certificate for marksmanship in the Junior Cadets Corps last week. That's worth a hundred namby-pamby Brownie badges.'

'Our badges aren't namby-pamby,' cried Helen hotly.

'Oh yes they are. Namby-pamby embroidery and making cups of tea.'

'You're wrong, Henry. Just listen to this!' Emily picked up the book. She wanted to read out some of the badges – the Survival badge for example – to show Henry how mistaken he was. But neither he nor his sister was in a listening mood.

'You won't find Junior Cadets skipping round in circles,' he was scoffing loudly. 'We have proper keep fit sessions every week.'

'Brownies keep fit,' argued Helen. 'I bet Em and I are a hundred times fitter than you.'

'OK, then. Prove it.'

They glared at each other.

'I know.' Henry jumped up from the table and pushed it against the wall. 'We'll have a contest – Brownies versus Junior Cadets.' He disappeared out through the door.

A few moments later he was struggling back in, with an ironing board under one arm and a plastic washing basket under the other.

'Just what do you think you're doing?' Helen demanded as he propped the board across two chairs and deposited the washing basket in the middle of the room.

Her brother leapt up on to the ironing board. 'Here we have an expanse of shark-infested ocean.' He pointed at the flower-patterned carpet. 'And here we have a rocky cliff path.' He swept his arm around the chairs, table and settee. 'Along which we race as far as this rope bridge.' He pointed down at the ironing board. 'From which we make a final dive into our trusty lifeboat.' He launched into the air and landed in the washing basket. 'Got it?'

'You mean you're challenging Helen to race round the furniture without touching the floor and end up in the washing basket,' Emily interpreted.

'Spot on. You time us. And the fittest is the one that does it fastest. Are you game, sis?'

'I'm game,' said Helen grimly.

'But what if your mum walks in?' Emily couldn't help asking.

'She'll be eaten by a shark,' Henry shrugged.

'Ha, ha. Very funny!' With a doubtful laugh Emily positioned herself in a corner and took off her watch. Fingers crossed – the contest would be over and the room back to normal before Mrs Hamilton got back.

'On your mark,' Henry called. 'Ready . . . steady . . . GO!'

Helen sprang into action. Sure-footed, she leapt from chair to chair. She scrambled on all fours across the table and plunged down on to a stool. From there she leapt on to the armchair to face the widest gap of all. Briefly she paused, measuring the distance. Then . . . yes! She'd done it. She was on the ironing board. One last leap and she had landed safely in the basket.

'Hurrah!' Emily cheered, caught up in the excitement of the moment. 'Twenty-nine seconds exactly.'

'Up the Junior Cadets. Twenty-nine seconds to beat.' Henry leapt on to the starting chair.

'Ready . . . steady . . . GO.'

He was off, clearing the first three chairs at break-neck speed, skidding across the table, hurling himself from the stool to the armchair to the ironing board.

'Twenty-one . . . twenty-two . . . twenty-three . .' Emily's voice rose.

He prepared for the final leap. And then – oops – his foot slipped . . .

'Henry!' shrieked Helen as – CRASH – he plunged down into the shark-infested water bringing the rope bridge with him and overturning the cliffs as he went.

'Are you all right?' The two girls rushed to help him to his feet.

He got up holding his hands to his face, muttering dazedly: 'I won. My time was fastest.'

'Look Emily! He's bleeding.' Helen went white.

Sure enough large splodges of bright red blood were dripping through Henry's fingers on to the ironing board.

'It's his nose. Go and get your mum,' ordered Emily. 'Come on, Henry. Into the kitchen. Quick!'

Half-pushing, half-steering, she guided the injured boy down the corridor. She didn't panic. And she didn't let Henry panic either – even though the front of his shirt was now covered in

lood. She made him put down his hands and
lean his head over the sink. 'People have loads of
blood inside them,' she said reassuringly, making him pinch his nose. 'So even though it *looks* as
f you're losing most of yours, you've still got
plenty left.'

'How do you know?' the boy croaked fearfully.

'Because you haven't passed out. And anyway
he bleeding's stopped!' Emily pointed out.

And with that Helen and her mum rushed in.
'You needn't worry, Mrs Hamilton. Henry's

had a bit of a nose-bleed. But everything's under control.'

It was a sadder wiser Junior Cadet who sat down at the tea-table that evening. 'You were great, Em,' he said gratefully. 'If it hadn't been for you I'd probably have bled all over the carpet and Mum would have stopped my pocket money for six months instead of a week. How did you know what to do?'

Emily and Helen exchanged glances.

'From the namby-pamby First Aid badge we did in Brownies last year.'

Henry hung his head. 'Oh . . . well . . . er . . . perhaps your badges aren't so namby-pamby after all,' he muttered. 'I was wrong. I'm sorry.'

'Never mind. You've actually done us a favour,' said Emily kindly.

'I have!' Henry looked surprised.

'That's right. You've helped us decide what badge to do next.' The girl looked across the kitchen at the blood-stained ironing board.

'Safety in the Home,' she beamed.

Emily and the Easter Chick

Emily's Brownie Pack had invited their nearest Brownie neighbours to join them for a Spring Fun Day. The Monday beforehand they sat in the Pow-Wow Ring, discussing the programme.

Karen put her fingers into the circle. 'Sometimes when we get together, we stick with our own Pack and don't make new friends,' she said. 'So I was wondering – you know how we said we would bring small Easter eggs to give to the visiting Brownies? Well, I wondered if each egg could have a name on it. And the Brownie who picks the egg with my name on will be my partner. And the one who picks the egg with Linda's name on will be Linda's partner. And so on. That way we'll all start getting to know each other right from the beginning.'

'Good thinking!' Mrs James nodded.

But there was more. Encouraged by the smiles and nods around the Ring, Karen suggested they made Easter chicks to hold their eggs. She'd even brought twenty-four knitting patterns showing how they could do it.

'Better and better!' Mrs James clapped with approval as the patterns were passed round.

Gloomily Emily stared at the piece of paper in her hand. She thought the idea was awful. It wasn't just that she didn't like knitting. The real problem was the way the Easter chicks were going to mix everyone up. New partners indeed! Emily didn't want a new partner. The only partner Emily wanted for the Fun Day was Sue.

She hoped Sue would feel the same way. While Karen explained how to sew up the chicks, the girl moved closer to her friend's side.

'Well, what do you think?' she whispered.

It was very disappointing to hear the enthusiasm in Sue's voice as she whispered back. 'I think it's a brilliant idea! Mum's got some yellow wool in her work-basket. I'm going to start knitting the minute I get home.'

'And what about the new partners?' Emily persisted.

'Sounds like a good way to make friends,' said Sue.

For the rest of the week Emily made a point of sighing and pouting every time the Fun Day was mentioned. Then on Friday Sue brought her chick into school. She had tucked a red Easter egg into its body, embroidered two black eyes on its head, added a red felt beak, and tied a little gold card with her name on round its neck. Even Emily forgot her disgust long enough to admit it looked sweet.

'So how's yours coming on then?' Sue asked.

There was a sulky silence.

'Don't you think you should get a move on? If you don't bring a chick to the Fun Day, you might end up with no partner.'

'I don't care! The only partner I want is you,' Emily snapped.

But she couldn't help thinking about what her friend had said. Eventually that evening, with the sort of a face which, according to her dad, made jokes sick, she got out her chick pattern.

Too late she discovered her mum didn't have much wool – just one grey ball left over from last year's school jumper.

'That'll have to do,' Emily pouted.

She brought the wool and a pair of knitting needles up to her bedroom and sat down on her bed. Casting on 34 stitches, she started to knit. By row six, four of the stitches had mysteriously disappeared. She didn't bother to look for them. She simply moved on to the second step of the pattern, adding five stitches to the next row to make up for the ones she had lost.

Forty finger-numbing minutes later she had finished the chick's head.

'At last!' She broke off the thread and drew it tightly through the last few stiches to form the neck.

All she had to do now was sew the thing up.

The pattern warned this could be tricky. After a further forty minutes Emily hurled her handiwork over the end of the bed in a rage. Sewing the chick up wasn't tricky – it was impossible.

She woke up at seven o'clock the next morning with Sue's words ringing in her memory. 'If you don't bring a chick to the Fun Day, you might end up with no partner.'

The thought spurred her into making one last determined effort. She rescued her tangled piece of knitting from the corner. She stretched. She tucked. She stitched. She pulled. And by breakfast time she had something vaguely bird-shaped beside her on the table.

'What's that supposed to be? A dead mouse?' Her dad peered over the top of the cereal packet.

'An Easter chick,' Emily rose with dignity. 'I still have to get an egg for it to sit on. Can I have my pocket money, please?'

A really nice egg would make her chick more lifelike, Emily tried to convince herself as she made her way to the corner shop.

'I want a small chocolate egg to go inside this chick, Mrs Robbins please,' she explained at the counter.

'Oh dear me!' The shopkeeper shook her head, dashing her hopes. 'I'm afraid I'm completely sold out of eggs that size.'

The visiting Pack arrived promptly. Two by two the Brownies came into the hall. Emily had positioned herself as far away from the display of Easter eggs as possible. But her eyes were still drawn to the table. None of the rest of her Pack seemed to have had any problems with their patterns. There the results sat – twenty-three little yellow chicks perched on gaily wrapped Easter eggs. And in the centre was her own clumsy effort, stretched almost to breaking point over a chocolate orange.

Mrs James, as always, had been kind. 'Appearances aren't important, Emily. You did your best. That's what counts.'

But Emily still wished she was a million miles away as she watched the visitors queuing to receive their chicks.

There was only one thing for it. She headed for the nearest Young Leader. 'Please, I need to go to the toilet,' she said.

Just as she had hoped the table was clear by

the time she came back. All over the hall pairs of Brownies sat completing their 'getting to know you' challenge. In the Pixie Six corner she could see Sue chatting happily to a new Brownie friend.

'Hello, you must be Emily.' A voice piped up at her side.

Emily turned round and found herself facing a freckle-faced Brownie with laughing grey eyes.

'I got your chick,' the Brownie continued. And held it up.

'Sorry about that. The shop had run out of Easter eggs,' Emily sighed.

'Sorry! What do you mean! I got twice as much chocolate as anyone else. I wish you'd come back sooner, though. We've only ten seconds left to tell each other all about ourselves. My name's Tessa, by the way. And you're Emily. And I've guessed a lot about you already. I guess you sometimes leave things to the last minute. And you're a bit shy, even though you don't look it. And you hate knitting.'

'Hey that's pretty good.' Emily grinned. 'I can tell a few things about you too.'

'Well?' Tessa raised her eyebrows.

If she had had longer there were all sorts of things Emily might have said. She might have said that she guessed Tessa was easy-going, with a great sense of fun, not afraid to speak her mind or do things her own way.

But Mrs James was holding up her arm for silence. There was just time for the briefest whisper.

'I can tell we're going to be friends,' Emily hissed.

Emily Gets into Trouble

Emily and Sue were on their way from the Brownie hall after a tidying-up Good Turn.

'Girls, come back a moment would you,' Mrs James called.

'She must want to thank us,' Emily grinned, as they turned round.

But if thanking them was what the Guider intended to do, she had a very funny way of going about it.

She didn't smile or pat their shoulders. She just stood there, looking at them. 'Is there anything you would like to tell me?' she asked.

What a strange question! 'I don't think so.' Emily shook her head. 'We stayed behind to brush the floor and put the chairs against the wall. But you know that.'

'And have you anything to tell me about what you did while I was out of the room?'

'We finished our Good Turn and left,' said Emily.

'You didn't go up on to the stage?'

The two friends looked at each other. A little warily, Sue replied. 'Well, yes. We did. Just for a second.'

'I was afraid of that.' Mrs James's expression, already serious, became grave. 'Come along with me.'

What was going on? Thoroughly puzzled the two girls followed their Guider back into the hall.

A strong smell of paint hit the girls as they came through the door. This in itself wasn't surprising. It was May – the month when the Dramatic Society put on their annual show. Earlier that evening, before the Meeting began, they had watched Mr Toplis, the artist responsible for the scenery, put the finishing touches to his handiwork. His backdrop of a green Austrian mountain-side complete with grazing cows and edelweiss had been brilliant. That was why they had popped on stage afterwards. It had seemed so lifelike from a distance, they couldn't resist going up for a closer look.

Mr Toplis was there again now . . . with a thunderous expression on his face.

'So these are the culprits!' He strode towards them. 'Well, girls, what have you got to say for yourselves?'

It seemed a lot of fuss about very little. Emily

frowned and said: 'We're sorry if you didn't want us looking at your scenery.'

'*Looking*!' The artist mopped the bald spot on the back of his grizzly head with a paint-stained handkerchief. 'I don't mind people *looking*. What I mind is *this*.' And with a firm hand on either girl's shoulder, he marched them up the steps and on to the stage.

The two Brownies found themselves standing at the bottom of a bank of artificial grass, in exactly the same spot as they had stood twenty minutes earlier. But what was this! Open-mouthed they saw that the bank looked as if it had been transformed into some sort of Austrian zebra crossing. It had a long wet stripe of white paint trickling down its middle.

'Oh dear!' gasped Emily. 'How did that happen?'

'You tell me. I left a can of paint sitting at the top of the bank when I went to wash my brushes,' Mr Toplis said grimly. 'My guess is that you and your little friend knocked it over. Then skipped off without a word to anyone.'

'No! No! We wouldn't do a thing like that!' cried Emily.

'Who did it then? One of those cows up there, eh? Or maybe the can just kicked up its heels and rolled over of its own accord? I'm sorry, girls, I've

watched enough amateur dramatics to know a fine bit of acting when I see one, so you can wipe those innocent expressions off your faces. You were to blame. And it's your parents who'll be footing the bill.'

'Ahem.' Mrs James placed a hand on his arm. 'I don't think we need involve anyone's parents. Since the accident happened in the course of a Brownie Meeting, the Brownies will pay for cleaning or replacing the bank out of funds.'

'Are you telling me you intend to let these little monkeys off the hook?' Mr Toplis rounded on her.

Mrs James turned first to Emily and then to Sue, looking them straight in the eyes. 'Are you sure you had nothing to do with the paint being spilt?'

'No. *Honestly.*'

'Very well. I believe you,' the Guider said. 'But you must never, on any account, go on to the stage again.'

Emily was furious.

'It isn't fair,' she fumed, the minute Mrs James and Mr Toplis were out of earshot. 'The only reason we stayed behind was to do a Good Turn. How dare that . . . that . . . bald-headed ape-man call us monkeys. He probably knocked over the can himself and then looked round for somebody else to blame!'

'Calm down, Em,' soothed Sue. 'Remember, Mrs James believed us.'

'She *said* she did, but . . . hey look!' Emily broke off. A figure, approaching at some speed down the path, had captured her attention. It was Mrs Nashe, the minister's wife. Her normally calm face seemed troubled.

'Is anything the matter, Mrs Nashe?' asked Sue.

'Oh, my dear. I'm looking for Tomkins. He always comes in for his tea at six o'clock. But this evening he didn't come home.'

'Perhaps there's been some emergency,' suggested Emily. 'Perhaps he was visiting one of the old people and they took sick and he had to take them to hospital . . .'

'I beg your pardon!' Mrs Nashe looked startled. Then she started to laugh. 'Oh, my dear! What a mix-up! Tomkins isn't my husband. He's my cat. I just wanted to check out the church grounds in case . . .'

'We'll keep our eyes open,' promised Sue. 'What does he look like?'

'He's black,' said Mrs Nashe. 'Jet black. And *very* handsome. I'm sorry. You must excuse me. I just hope he's all right . . .' And she hurried off down the path calling 'Tomkins! Tomkins!' in an anxious fluting tone.

'Poor Mrs Nashe,' said Sue. 'She sounds really worried. Wouldn't it be great if we could find her pet for her?'

'I suppose so,' Emily shrugged, secretly feeling she'd had enough of Brownie Good Turns for one day.

But her friend was determined. 'Tomkins! Tomkins!' she kept calling across fences and hedges as they set off for home.

'That doesn't sound right,' said Emily grumpily. 'You need to call him like this. "Tomkins! Tomkins!"' She gave an exaggerated impression of Mrs Nashe's fluting tone.

Nobody could have been more surprised when a cat bounded out of the hedgerow at her feet.

'Tomkins!' cried Sue.

For a split second Emily thought so too. Then she took a second look. 'No it's not.' Gently with the end of her toe, she prodded the animal back into the hedge. 'Tomkins is jet black. That moggy has a big white patch on one side.'

'What a pity!' Sue sighed.

But Emily wasn't listening. She was staring at her shoe – at the sticky white stain where her toe had come into contact with the stray cat's fur.

Next minute, to Sue's amazement, she was diving into the hedge.

'That *was* Tomkins,' she gasped. 'And we really

really need to catch him to clear our names. Just
watch your uniform if you pick him up, Sue. He's
covered in white paint.'

Five minutes later there was a grand reunion
back in the hall.

'Oh; Tomkins! You naughty, naughty pussy!'
Mrs Nashe cuddled her pet with a fine disregard
for the state of her jacket. 'Imagine knocking
over a nasty can of paint and ruining dear Mr
Toplis's beautiful bank just when he had made

116

everything perfect. Girls, I am so very grateful. And Mr Toplis, I am so very sorry.'

For the second time that evening, the artist mopped his bald spot.

'Nothing that a bottle of white spirit and a can of green spray won't fix,' he muttered sheepishly.

Well! Emily and Sue exchanged glances. It had been a different story when he'd thought *they* were to blame.

Still at least they'd made it up to Mrs Nashe for a certain mix-up at the last Guide sale.

And Mr Toplis obviously regretted his mistake.

'Here you are, girls.' He slipped a couple of envelopes into their hands. 'No hard feelings?'

Delighted, the Brownies pulled out two free show tickets.

'Oh, thank you, Mr Toplis. No. No hard feelings at all.'

A Thief at Blinkthorn Manor

It was on the very first outing of the Pack Holiday that disaster struck.

Up until that moment everything had been wonderful. 'This is going to be our best Pack Holiday ever! I just know it!' Emily had told Sue happily as they arrived. She'd been full of excitement. First because the place they were staying in, Blinkthorn Manor, was such a big, old, interesting house. And second because there was an enormous funfair half a mile down the road.

She'd been more excited than ever when Mrs James had announced that their first outing would be a walk into Blinkthorn to see it. 'A pity the village is so touristy,' Emily overheard her say to Miss Lappin the Assistant Guider, when they reached the top of Blinkthorn hill. Emily didn't agree. In her eyes the village below, with its coloured lights, its funfair, its gift shops and ice-cream vans, was one step away from paradise.

She did agree, though, that it was a pity the narrow streets were so crowded. People seemed to be visiting the village in their thousands that afternoon. 'We'll need to divide into groups so that no one gets lost,' Mrs James said. 'Make your way to the car park, Brownies, and we'll get ourselves organised.'

And that was when it happened – the disaster.

Miss Lappin was helping Mrs James shepherd the Pack across the road, looking calm, smart and capable in her navy culottes one minute, and the next she was down on her hands and knees, clutching her shoulder, shouting at the top of her voice.

'Stop! Stop! Thief!'

Of course they couldn't visit the shops or the funfair after that. It wasn't just that Miss Lappin had got a nasty cut on her knee and needed to be taken straight back to the house to have it washed and bandaged. Even if she had been right as rain, there wouldn't have been any point in staying. Her bag had been snatched. And the Brownie Pocket Money Bank – all one hundred pounds of it – had been inside.

'I brought the money downstairs to give to Mrs Dove to put in the safe. And then I forgot. And now it's gone. Every penny!' the Guider kept on repeating. First to Mrs James, then to a police

119

officer and finally, when they got back to the Manor, to Mrs Dove, the warden.

Emily hung about in the background, eavesdropping shamelessly.

'It's awful. We might as well go and stay on a desert island now,' she moaned to Sue that evening. 'At least there we wouldn't have to spend the rest of the week looking at things we couldn't buy.'

Usually bedtime on the first night of Pack Holiday was a riot. Everybody bounced on beds and raced in and out of the washrooms, and talked until three in the morning.

But that night was different. The Brownies were very subdued. Emily knew they were probably all thinking the same thing – no ice-creams – no presents – no rides on the Big Wheel. Pack Holiday wouldn't be Pack Holiday without pocket money.

Surely there was *something* they could do. *Bong. Bong. Bong.* The grandfather clock in the entrance hall struck midnight and the girl lay awake in her cosy bunk-bed, racking her brains. Suddenly she sat bolt upright, a determined frown on her face. Leaning over the side of the bed she prodded the figure below.

'Sue! Sue! Get up quick and wake the rest of the Six,' she whispered. 'I've had an idea.'

Not everyone was altogether delighted to be summoned to the washroom at that hour of the morning.

'I don't know what this is about, Em,' hissed Linda sternly, 'but it had better be important. Mrs James has enough on her plate without you adding to her worries.'

Emily looked hurt. 'My plan is to give Mrs James less worries – not more. I think I know how we can get back the stolen bag.'

'Oh yes?' Linda raised her eyebrows.

'It's really simple,' Emily dropped her voice to a whisper. 'All we have to do is hide behind the curtains in the entrance hall and wait for the thief.'

'And snatch the bag back as he slips past, I suppose. Come off it, Emily. There isn't one chance in a million the thief will come snooping around here.'

'Oh but you're wrong, Linda,' Emily cried earnestly. 'Just remember. As well as the money, he got the Manor keys. Mrs Dove gave all three Guiders a set. Look at it this way: if you were a thief, which would you choose to burgle, a house you had to break into, or one where you could just unlock the front door and stroll in?'

'Yes, well, the one where I had the keys, I suppose,' Linda muttered.

'Exactly.' Emily knew she had made her point.

Half-an-hour later, though, as she stood with the rest of the Six squashed behind the entrance hall curtains, the point wasn't so clear. It was cold and dark and spooky in the entrance hall.

'This is a waste of time. I think we should go back to bed,' Linda shivered.

Deep down Emily was beginning to feel the same way. But she didn't intend to admit it. 'Please. Just another ten minutes,' she begged.

Everyone shifted restlessly, and then, suddenly . . . scrunch . . . scrunch . . . scrunch . . .

'Footsteps!' Sue hissed. 'Footsteps across the gravel. He's *coming*!'

Clutching each other, they heard the sound of keys being inserted in the lock. They had only a few seconds to prepare.

'Linda, Karen and Helen, you grab his legs from behind. Sue and I will sit on his shoulders. And Jill, you wake Mrs Dove and get her to ring the police,' ordered Emily.

With scarcely a creak the front doors of Blinkthorn Manor swung open. A shadowy figure crept into the hall.

'Now!' Emily gave the sign and the Pixies swung into action.

'Eow! Argh! Gerroff!'

The operation was a complete success. Within

seconds the intruder had been floored and lay pinned to the carpet, helplessly flapping his leather-jacketed arms. 'Eow! Help! Gerroff!' he continued to yell.

The noise saved Jill the trouble of waking Mrs Dove.

'Who is it? What's going on down there?' the warden called from the landing.

'It's only us – the Pixies,' Emily called back, bouncing down hard on the intruder's shoulders to keep him under control. 'We've caught the thief,' bounce, 'the one who stole Miss Lappin's bag.'

'Have you indeed?' Mrs Dove had switched on the lights by this time, and came tripping down the stairs, a small yet commanding figure in her sporty night attire. On the bottom step she paused, her hands on her hips.

'Well I never!' She burst out laughing.

'Ouf! Quick! Get them off me!' the thief yelled.

It was all very embarrassing. So embarrassing Emily would cheerfully have gone straight back to her own house and never set eyes on Blinkthorn Manor again. Of course there'd been no question of calling the police. Their thief had turned out to be Mrs Dove's reporter son, Leo, coming home from a late-night assignment.

Fortunately he hadn't broken any bones. He had been bruised. But not too bruised to sit down and interview Linda, who'd left him in no doubt about the ringleader of the ambush.

This was fair enough, Emily supposed, back in her bunk-bed once more. If you were going to bounce up and down on the shoulders of a perfectly respectable young reporter for no good reason, you couldn't turn round and ask him not to write about it in his newspaper. But still, it wasn't going to be Linda or Karen or Sue who would be made the laughing-stock, it would be *her*.

With a groan, the girl tried to put the whole unfortunate incident out of her mind and get some sleep. But she kept imagining the newspaper headlines: 'MEET EMILY – THE BROWNIE BULLY OF BLINKTHORN,' or 'HOUSEHOLDERS BEWARE – EMILY COULD BE BEHIND *YOUR* CURTAINS.'

It was one very miserable, heavy-eyed Brownie who got up to face the world next morning.

'Emily,' said Mrs James, 'you look exhausted. I think you'd better go straight back to bed.'

Perhaps I'm sick, the girl thought hopefully as she climbed back under the duvet.

She woke up some four hours later to the sound of cheers in the playroom below.

'Oh dear!' She curled up with embarrassment as the memories came flooding back. 'Everyone's laughing. I bet it's at me.'

And with that Sue burst in, waving a copy of the *Blinkthorn Gazette*.

'Emily! Emily! Guess what?'

'Don't tell me!' Emily disappeared down under the duvet so that only her eyes and the top of her head could be seen.

'Leo Dove's written this article about us. All about Mrs James's bag being stolen and how all our pocket money was lost.'

'An article about our pocket money!' Slowly, very slowly, Emily sat herself up. 'Here, let me see.'

Scarcely daring to breathe she started to read. 'SNEAK THIEF SPOILS BROWNIES' FUN' was the headline. She let her breath out. What a relief! There wasn't a single mention of last night.

'In the last half an hour the phone's never stopped ringing,' Sue continued excitedly. 'There're people wanting to give us money and people wanting to give us ice-cream and the fairground people rang up to say they wanted to give the whole Pack free rides.'

Free rides! Emily was out of bed like a shot, shedding her embarrassment with the bedclothes.

'Of course I knew all along it was the right thing to hide behind the curtains,' she exclaimed happily as she leapt down the stairs towards the playroom. 'That's often the way it is with my ideas – I know what to do without quite knowing why.'

'And we do what you tell us without knowing why either. Crazy, isn't it?' smiled Sue.

Emily and the River Den

Two weeks before the parents' evening something terrible happened. The boiler in St Mark's
church exploded. For a few days it looked as if the
1st Hammington Brownies would have nowhere
to meet. Then the Scouts came to the rescue.

'They have very kindly given us the use of their
River Den for as long as we need it,' Mrs James
explained to the Brownies the following Monday
as the Brownies explored the new premises. 'So
you can tell your mums and dads that the
parents' evening will be held as planned this day
week – at the River Den.' She smiled cheerfully.
'Now, let's get down to business.'

The final rehearsal got underway. One after
another the Sixes stood up in front of the rest of
the Pack to practise their items: the Gnomes did
their folk dances, the Elves recited, the Kelpies
did keep fit and the Pixies mimed their nursery
rhymes . . . but somehow, even though everyone
more or less knew what they were doing – nobody

tripped, or forgot their words or got tangled up in a skipping-rope – something was missing. 'There isn't much "oomph" about this year's programme,' Emily overheard Mrs James sigh.

On her way home, the girl considered the problem. In her opinion the River Den was to blame. The Scouts had said they didn't use it much in the winter, and Emily could see why. It had none of the bright solid comfort of their own hall. It was a bare, wooden, prefabricated barn of a building, guaranteed to dampen any performance.

Still, that was no excuse for not trying, Emily knew. 'I wonder how we can get more "oomph" into our nursery rhymes?' she asked herself. 'Hey wait a minute, I've thought of something.' Her eyes lit up.

Talking people into agreement took a lot of hard work. First she had to convince Sue and then she had to convince Linda and finally she had to convince Mrs James.

'Little Miss Muffet is a bore,' she argued. 'Nobody gets excited about someone in an apron and a frilly bath-cap running away from a plastic spider. But Old Mother Hubbard with a real live dog called Nipper would be a sensation.'

'I'll tie him up in the store,' she promised. 'He'll just come out for the mime and then go straight back into the store again.'

'He's such a quiet, obedient dog,' she stressed. 'He always does what I tell him and he begs beautifully. Honestly.'

In the end she got her way.

'I can see you have your heart set on this, Emily,' said Mrs James. 'So yes, I give you permission to act Old Mother Hubbard with Nipper.'

The following Monday night, arriving at the River Den, Emily felt sure the evening would go well. She felt more certain than ever when she stepped inside. The place still smelt musty, but it was full of parents. Eight rows of heads turned to stare as she walked in with her pet. Nipper, for his part, looked every inch a star. His tail wagged cockily and he had a big blue bow tied under his collar.

'I know you'll be brilliant.' She fondled the terrier's ears as she led him into the store. 'Just remember – no barking, especially during prayers.' She attached his lead to a convenient hook and ran out to join the rest of the Pack.

The programme began smoothly. Mrs James made her welcoming speech and the Gnomes tripped out into the centre of the floor for their dances. It was only then it became clear that the River Den's dampening effect was still at work.

'Oh help!' whispered Linda.

'What's got into them?' wondered Sue.

130

Emily decided they must be nervous. That was the only explanation for all the mistakes. First they missed their entry. Then they forgot their steps. It was hard to believe they were the same group who had danced perfectly (if dully) at the rehearsal only the week before.

Everyone heaved a sigh of relief when they finally got to the end of the item. There was a polite round of applause, and the Elves came on.

If the Gnomes had been nervous, the Elves were scared stiff. The previous Monday they had recited clearly (if dully), but tonight they just mumbled into the front of their T-shirts.

'Speak up!' hissed Linda.

'Have they started yet?' wondered Sue.

Some of the parents seemed to be wondering the same thing. One or two were even beginning to chat amongst themselves, when CRASH. A burst of sound made everyone jump. It came from the store. Barking. Yapping. Growling. The sound of a terrier going wild.

'Shhh. Bad dog. Be quiet, Nipper.' Emily raced towards the back of the hall.

Of course she ought to have smelt a rat. She ought to have known that Nipper wouldn't make such a fuss about nothing. But she was so concerned about the parents' evening, she didn't stop

to think. She just flung open the door, and the ra
– a real live brown one – shot out.

Pandemonium reigned. Half the parents stood
on their chairs and screamed. The other hal
froze in open-mouthed horror. A couple of Young
Leaders, armed with brushes, joined Nipper (who
had just snapped his lead) chasing the rat round
the room.

'Out! Out!' Mrs James yelled and opened the
front door.

Out they all streamed – the rat, followed by Nipper, followed by Emily, followed by the Young Leaders.

Things calmed down after that. By the time the three girls had hauled the dog out of the river and dragged him back into the Den, Mrs James had everyone sitting in their seats again, and the Pixies, dressed in their nursery rhyme costumes, were taking the floor.

Emily had a bare thirty seconds to get ready for her act.

At home, that afternoon, she and Nipper had given a faultless performance. Dressed in a big white apron with a shawl round her shoulders, Emily had begun the mime by sweeping the floor. At a whispered command, Nipper had tugged at her skirt and begged. He had continued to beg appealingly as Emily pretended to search for a bone, high up, low down. Her final sad shake of the head had been the signal for him to roll over on his back and waggle his paws in the air.

'Charming! Really charming! I have to hand it to you, Emily. You have that dog well-trained,' her mum had clapped.

Now was the moment when eight rows of parents were supposed to be equally impressed.

'Come on.' With her apron half-tied and her shawl half-on Emily hauled her bedraggled pet

into the middle of the room. Her broom had disappeared in the rat-chasing episode so she couldn't pretend to sweep. 'Beg, Nipper,' she hissed, letting go of the dog's collar. But instead of begging Nipper raced off into a corner and started sniffing along the side of the room.

Never in Emily's worst dreams had she thought this could happen. 'Beg, Nipper,' she pleaded, hauling him back. It was no good. Nipper had no intention of playing his part in the nursery rhyme. All he wanted to do was hunt rats, and all Emily could do in the end was pick him up in her arms and retire to the store.

The item for which she had had such high hopes had been a flop.

She stayed in the store for the rest of the programme. 'I can't leave Nipper. He's too upset,' she told Linda when the Sixer came to get her for orange juice and biscuits.

A few moments later Mrs James put her head round the door.

'I believe Nipper's upset,' she said. 'Do you know why?'

Emily hung her head. 'He's really ashamed of himself,' she sighed.

'Ashamed of himself!' Mrs James sounded amazed. 'But that's ridiculous. You saw for yourself how nervous everyone was to begin with. His

rat-hunt was the turning point in the programme. It broke the ice. Gave everyone a
chance to warm up.'

Emily's frown lifted slightly. She knelt down
and retied her pet's muddy bow. Of course she
knew Mrs James was probably just being kind,
but still . . .

'A turning point! Did you hear that, Nipper?'
she whispered.

'Woof.' Nipper caught hold of her skirt and
tugged.

Outside the store eight rows of parents sat
finishing their tea and biscuits. Emily had hoped
to slip past quietly, but Nipper had other ideas.
He gave a second sharp little bark – as if to
attract attention – then sat up on his hind legs to
beg.

'Sorry, doggie, the cupboard is bare,' somebody
called.

'The rats beat you to it,' somebody else shouted.

There was a burst of laughter, and Emily
couldn't help joining in. Yes, she could see it now
– see it in eight rows of smiling faces. Mrs James
had been right. The evening was a success. There
was nothing to be ashamed of. Nothing at all.

Nipper had added 'oomph' to the show.

A Slip-up at the Sale

In September Emily got a new teacher. Her name was Miss Watt. Emily really liked her. She was fair. She didn't shout much. And she was an Assistant Guider in the Guide Unit.

At the end of the month the Unit decided to hold a sale to raise funds for equipment.

'I hear the Brownies are helping us at the sale tomorrow,' Miss Watt said to Emily in class.

'Yes. We're selling cakes and plants,' Emily nodded.

Miss Watt opened her arithmetic book with a smile. 'I'll bake a cake for your stall,' she promised. 'Let's hope people will know it's meant to be eaten, not put in a pot.'

Some teachers might have forgotten that kind of promise, made so lightly between library-time and sums, but not Miss Watt.

'I have my cake all iced and ready,' she told Emily on the day of the sale. 'There's just one problem. I've an appointment with the headmaster at four o'clock today, so I may be a bit late getting down to the church hall. If I leave it in a box on my doorstep, do you think you could collect it?'

'Of course, Miss Watt,' said Emily happily. 'Linda and I are going straight to the hall after school.'

Miss Watt's house was only a minute's walk away from the church. Sure enough the two girls could see a cake-box sitting on the doorstep when they turned in through the gate. But there was something else as well.

'Gosh! They must be for the plant stall.' Linda let out her breath in a gasp of admiration. 'Aren't they beautiful! I didn't know Miss Watt could arrange flowers.'

Emily looked at the arrangement of red roses in their pearl-trimmed basket. 'Miss Watt is always taking us by surprise,' she said, carefully gripping the handle so as not to disturb its satin bow. 'That's why we've nicknamed her Watt-Next.'

'Watt-Next.' The Sixer nodded approvingly. 'I like that. Our class is still struggling to get a nickname for our new teacher, Mr Pendlebury. So far we can't get anything to stick.'

They continued to chew over possible nicknames for Linda's teacher all the way to the church hall.

138

The Brownie stall was already well filled with cakes and plants when they came in with their contributions.

'Good for you, girls. Cakes to the left. Plants to the right,' Mrs James came over waving a roll of price-tags.

'These flowers are so nice I think they should go right in the middle,' suggested Emily. Everyone agreed. But no sooner had the display been given this central position on the table than Mrs Nashe, the minister's wife, came along.

'Well I never – if that isn't the very thing I'm looking for,' she cried. 'I promised to organise a floral arrangement for a concert this evening and that basket of roses would be absolutely perfect. Would you mind selling it before the sale opens?'

'Of course we'll sell it,' said Linda happily. So Miss Watt's roses were passed across the table to Mrs Nashe who promptly transferred them on to a pedestal on the stage.

Business was brisk on the Brownie stall. Emily sold two geraniums and three packets of seeds before she noticed something lying in the gap between an azalea and a cherry log.

She picked it up.

A moment later she gave a cry of dismay. 'Oh dear, Linda! Wait till you see this!'

But Linda's attention was elsewhere. 'Look!'

she pointed. 'There's Mr Pendlebury stopping to admire Miss Watt's flowers. Sir! Sir!' she called out before Emily could stop her, 'do you want a cactus?'

Mr Pendlebury headed towards them. He was a young, dark-haired man with glasses and a very slight stutter, which was only noticeable when he got worked up.

He was stuttering now.

'N-no thanks. But those f-f-flowers, d-do you know where they c-c-came from?'

'Oh yes,' began Linda.

'The florist,' Emily interrupted. 'They came from the florist. Mrs Nashe wanted a professional arrangement for her concert tonight. Oh dear! I see what you mean. They do look a bit limp. Excuse us, sir.' She grabbed her friend's arm. 'We'd better take them out and water them.'

But instead of heading to the kitchen, Linda discovered they were heading out of the main door.

'Just *what* do you think you're playing at, Emily?' she demanded. 'We can't just walk off with these roses. Mrs Nashe will have a fit if she sees.'

'We'll worry about her later,' said Emily. 'Right now we have to get them back to Miss Watt. Fast!' And she sprinted off down the path.

'Save the questions,' she panted over her shoulder. 'I can explain everything, just as long as we're in time. Yes. Thank goodness!' She caught sight of the teacher's Mini Metro parked outside her house. 'Watt-Next has only just got back from school. Now you wait in the bushes while I make the delivery.'

More bewildered than ever, Linda watched the younger girl dash up to the door and deposit the basket.

A few seconds passed – just long enough for Emily to dash back into the bushes. Then the door opened and Miss Watt, dressed in her Guider's uniform, stepped out. As she spotted the roses, her face lit up. She lifted the basket carefully and brought it inside.

Linda looked at Emily and swallowed.

'I think I'm beginning to understand now, Em,' she said slowly. 'Those flowers weren't meant for our plant stall, were they?'

'Nope.' Emily shook her head.

'They were a present to Miss Watt.'

'Right.' Emily nodded.

'From . . . No! I don't believe it!'

'Shh . . . keep your voice down.'

A second car had pulled up outside the house and a young dark-haired man got out.

'Mr Pendlebury!' Linda had to stuff her fists

into her mouth to stop herself giggling out loud. This set Emily off, and next thing both girls were rolling around in the bushes in an agony of silent laughter. The most shriek-making moment of all came when they heard Miss Watt open the door: 'Yes, of course I got them, darling. They're absolutely gorgeous,' she cried. Then, hand in hand, the two teachers came walking down the path towards the car.

'Oh Watt-Next? Watt-Next?' Linda gasped between gales of merriment, as the car pulled away from the pavement with Mr Pendlebury in the passenger seat. 'Emily, how did you guess?'

'There was a little card in the roses. It must have been tucked away so we didn't see it at first, but then it fell out and I found it lying on the stall. *All my love, Vincent*, it said. I knew as soon as I saw Mr Pendlebury staring at the flowers, they had to be from him.'

'And to think we sold them to Mrs Nashe!' Suddenly Linda's grin faded slightly. 'Oh dear . . . Mrs Nashe!'

'We'd better go back now and refund her money,' Emily wiped the tears from her eyes. 'And explain the flowers weren't ours to sell.'

'What a mix-up!' Linda nodded. But her grin was back. 'Still, at least Mr Pendlebury's got his nickname at long last . . .'

'Well come on, let's hear it?'

'All-My-Love-Vincent!'

'All-My-Love-Vincent! Oh . . . Oh . . .' Emily spluttered.

And the two girls collapsed in fits of laughter on the grass.

Emily Sends for the Doctor

Walking from Emily's house to Sue's house took five minutes, if she turned left at the end of her road, then cut down a little path alongside a row of terraced houses.

The end house in the row was the house where Mrs Honey lived. It was hard to see how anyone could be afraid of Mrs Honey. She was a small neat elderly woman who looked as sweet as her name. But Emily *was* afraid of her – so afraid she preferred to spend an extra ten minutes trudging along the main road to her friend's, rather than run the risk of bumping into the old lady as she passed her front door. Of course she couldn't tell anyone why. It all sounded so stupid.

Then came the Saturday morning when her mum told her to be home from Sue's at one o'clock *sharp*.

'But it's only twenty to one. You can get back to your house in five minutes!' Sue protested when she saw her friend putting on her coat.

'Not any more I can't,' said Emily. There was no getting out of it then. She had to explain.

'You're joking. You can't be afraid of Mrs Honey!' Sue cried.

'She might look like a sweet little old lady when you meet her in the street,' Emily argued. 'But she turns into another person the minute she closes her front door.'

Sue raised her eyebrows disbelievingly.

'What do you make of this, then?' Emily rose to the challenge. 'A few weeks ago I was passing Mrs Honey's on my way here. Her kitchen window was open. Just as I went past I heard something really creepy, the sort of horrible cackling laugh a witch would give. So I decided to take a quick peek inside.' She paused.

'Go on. What did you see?' Sue was interested now.

'I saw Mrs Honey with her back to me,' Emily continued slowly, 'standing beside the cooker stirring a huge big saucepan. And then I heard the cackling, louder and horribler and creepier than ever.' She shivered at the memory. 'That was when I made up my mind not to go past her house any more.'

'Well,' said Sue sensibly. 'You'd better go past it today. You've taken so long telling me the story, you'll be late for lunch if you don't. But

never mind. All you have to do is run straight past the house. No matter how creepily she cackles, Mrs Honey's hardly likely to leap out and grab you, now is she?'

'No I suppose not,' Emily agreed.

It was a relief to have told someone. Sue's sensible advice helped Emily feel brave as she approached the terrace. Mrs Honey's house looked just the same as ever. No coloured smoke rising from the chimney. No suspicious smells drifting from the kitchen.

'All I have to do is run past,' the girl reminded herself. She took a deep breath and started to sprint along the path.

But what was that? As she passed the kitchen window, a voice halted her progress. She stood for a moment, listening intently. Yes, there it was again. A hoarse pleading cry.

'Help me! Help me!'

Oh dear! Emily's heart pounded. Mrs Honey had had an accident. She was calling for help. And then a horrible thought struck her. Perhaps it was a trick. Perhaps it was the old woman's way of drawing her inside?

'Help me! Help me!'

Should she? Shouldn't she? The girl remembered the bubbling saucepan. And made up her mind. 'You won't put me in your brew, Honeybun,' she muttered and ran off as fast as she could.

By the time she'd reached the road though, she was having second thoughts. What if the cry for help was genuine? What if Mrs Honey had fallen over and had been lying on the kitchen floor for hours?

'I'll get Mum to ring Dr Webb as soon as I get home,' Emily decided.

But there was a phone box just up the road and obviously if Mrs Honey *had* had an accident it was important to get help as quickly as possible. The girl changed direction. A few seconds later she was lifting the receiver, shoving a twenty pence piece through the slot and dialling her doctor's number.

'Hello, Dr Webb? This is Emily Martin,' she gasped. 'It's a bit of an emergency. I was passing 28 Apple-Tree Terrace . . . yes, that's Mrs Honey's house, and I heard someone calling for help. Can you come round straight away? Oh good! Thanks a million, Dr Webb. What's that? Oh, I don't think I could . . . well, all right then, I'll do my best.'

The girl hung up, frowning and gnawing her lower lip. What had she let herself in for? She had just promised Dr Webb she would cover Mrs Honey with a blanket and comfort her until he arrived.

Gingerly, very gingerly, Emily approached the front door. It wasn't locked. More gingerly than ever she poked her head inside.

'Mrs Honey! It's Emily Martin,' she quavered. 'Are you all right?'

No answer. The hallway was silent – unnaturally silent – creepily still.

Only her promise to Dr Webb stopped Emily slamming the door and running away.

'Mrs Honey! Mrs Honey!' Emily quavered, edging her way along the wall towards the kitchen.

Not a word. Nothing except the ticking of the clock on the wall. Tick . . . tock . . . tick . . . tock. Emily tiptoed round the corner.

'Ha-ha-ha-ha!' A burst of raucous laughter hit her like a slap in the face.

'Oh no! Help!' she screamed.

'Who's a pretty girl then?' came the cackling voice. 'Ha-ha-ha-ha! Who's a pretty girl?'

Emily clapped her hand to her mouth and stared, almost dizzy with relief. She understood now. There was nothing to be afraid of. Nothing at all. Then she remembered Dr Webb rushing away from his lunch in answer to her call. 'Oh dear. I feel so stupid,' she murmured aloud.

'Would you like to tell me why?' a kindly voice inquired behind her.

And spinning round, Emily found herself face to face with Mrs Honey.

Fortunately the old lady was very understanding. And so was Dr Webb when he came. 'For every emergency, we've a dozen false alarms,' he said cheerfully, when he discovered there was no need for the ambulance after all. 'You did the right thing, young lady.'

Emily looked at the clock. 'I hope Mum sees it that way.'

'Well, perhaps this will sweeten your story.' Mrs Honey handed her a pot of marmalade. 'You can tell her it's home-made.'

Emily looked at the marmalade. Then she looked across at the cage beside the cooker, where Polly, Mrs Honey's talkative, brilliantly feathered parrot, sat preening herself on her perch. How easy it was to get the wrong impression.

'I know. I saw you making it.' She took the pot with a smile.

'Help me! Who's a pretty girl then! Ha-ha-ha-ha!' the parrot squawked.

Emily and the Blue Bucket

'This kitchen is hopeless.' Emily shut the fridge door and sat down. 'Karen's bringing Danish pastries. And Sue's bringing Italian pasta and Linda's bringing Indian tea and Helen's bringing Belgian chocolates and Jill's bringing Dutch cheese – and what am I bringing? Nothing. Because there's nothing in our kitchen to bring . . .' She glared accusingly at her mother.

Mrs Martin frowned. 'If only you'd mentioned it sooner,' she murmured.

'Mentioned what?' a voice called, and Mr Martin strode through the door. 'Oops. I get it.' He looked from his wife to his daughter and pretended to zip up his lips. 'If you want to stay on goods terms with the family, don't ask.'

'I'll tell you anyway,' sighed Mrs Martin. 'As usual Emily has left things to the last minute. Five minutes ago she announced she had to bring some food from another country where there are Brownies for a Brownies-Round-the-World evening tonight. Now she's moaning because she can't find anything to bring. I mean, what does she expect? A fridge full of beansprouts? I'm in the business of feeding a family, not running a Chinese takeaway!'

Thoughtfully Ron Martin rubbed his chin. 'So what do we have in stock then?'

'The usual things – cornflakes, carrots, custard powder, potatoes . . .'

'Hmmm.' The tall man was as dark as his daughter was fair, but their eyes lit up in exactly the same way when they had a brainwave. 'Anyone know if there are Brownies in Peru?'

Emily glanced at the phone. 'I could ring and ask Mrs James, I suppose. But what's the point?' She bit her lip. 'I can't think of anything from Peru except llamas – and we don't have one of those in the fridge.'

'Abracadabra.' Her father gave a fairy godmother-like flap of his arms. 'No, seriously, I've had an idea. Listen . . .' He beckoned Emily over to the vegetable rack. It took a bit of explaining. But in the end he managed to convince the worried Brownie that her problem was solved.

Half-an-hour later she walked slowly into the Brownie hall.

'There you are at last,' Linda was in their Six corner helping Jill label an array of foodstuffs.

154

'We were afraid you weren't coming. Did you remember to bring something for the display?'

'Of course.' Emily had been standing with her hands behind her back, but now she swung her contribution into full view – a blue plastic bucket full of potatoes.

'Um . . . what country do we put on those? Cyprus?' Jill asked doubtfully.

'No. Ireland. It's Ireland, isn't it, Emily?' said Sue.

Emily sighed. She was beginning to wish her dad had kept his brainwave to himself.

'I brought potatoes to remind us of Brownies in Peru,' she announced more knowledgeably than she felt.

'*Peru!*'

'Yes. That's where they come from. Historically, I mean. The Spaniards discovered the first potatoes in the Andes mountains when they went there in the sixteenth century.'

'Good for them!' shrugged Karen.

'At least it's a nice short name.' Jill lifted her pen.

'A whole bucketful of potatoes won't look very nice. Let's just pick out a small one for the display,' said Helen.

Something about the way they spoke annoyed Emily.

'The Spaniards didn't just bring *one* potato back from Peru, you know. And it jolly well took a lot of effort to lug that lot from the house.' Her voice shook.

'Here, let me help you lift the bucket on to the table,' soothed Linda quickly.

The next minute Mrs James held up her hand for silence.

Unhappily Emily trailed after the rest of the Pixies into the Brownie Ring. She was kicking herself. Obviously she was going to spend the whole evening explaining the connection between potatoes and Peru. Why, oh why hadn't she remembered the Challenge in time to bring something straightforward – like a stick of French bread.

To make matters worse Mrs James had a visitor with her that night – an attractive auburn-haired woman with glasses.

'This is Miss Porter,' the Guider announced after prayers. 'She's what is known as a Trainer – and before you ask, Helen – no, that doesn't mean she trains horses. The training she organises is for Brownie Guiders, to help them run Brownie Packs. So now, if you'll just go back into your Six corners for a moment, I'll bring her round to look at your displays.'

As the adults turned to leave the Ring, somehow Miss Porter caught her foot in the strap of Miss Lappin's bag. 'Ooops,' she stumbled forwards. Oh dear! Her glasses flew off the bridge of her nose on to the floor. She picked them up only to discover that one lens was broken.

'Not to worry. I've a spare pair at home,' she reassured the watching Brownies. 'Just go on into your corners, everyone.'

She proceeded to accompany Mrs James on her tour around the hall. But despite her cheerful attitude, she obviously couldn't see very well. Instead of taking the sort of knowledgeable interest you might expect a Brownie Trainer to take in the various items, all she could do was smile vaguely and murmur 'very nice' at every table.

And then she reached the Pixie Corner.

There – suddenly – she stopped, pointing. 'Do I see what I think I see. Could that be a blue bucket of potatoes?' she cried.

'Emily'll explain.' Linda pushed Emily forward.

Emily took a deep breath. 'The potatoes are there to remind us of –' She broke off. Miss Porter wasn't listening. Her strangely naked eyes were shining. She clasped the astonished Brownie by the hands. 'What a lovely surprise. I suppose Mrs James must have told you and you brought it specially. How very clever!'

If she had banged her head in her fall, there would have been a clear reason for this odd behaviour. As it was, all Emily could do was nod and smile back and wonder, with the rest of the Six, what on earth she had done to send the Trainer into such waves of delight.

They didn't have to wait long to find out.

Miss Porter moved from their Six corner to the centre of the hall, smiling brightly and holding up her hand to show she was about to make a speech.

'It has been a very great pleasure to meet you all,' she said. 'I have been most impressed by your work, and the trouble you have gone to to find out about Brownies in other parts of the world. As Mrs James may have told you, I have just returned from a trip into the middle of the Atlantic Ocean, to the island of St Helena. And it has given me the greatest thrill imaginable to see that at least one Brownie here has remembered the Brownies there.' She paused, and beamed at Emily. 'For those of you who don't know, if you were a Brownie living on St Helena, you would almost certainly own a blue bucket. Blue buckets used to come to the island filled with lard. The islanders saved them and still use them in much the same way as we use plastic bags. Emily, I don't know how you found out about that. But

159

congratulations on a wonderful piece of research!'

Emily blushed bright red. 'Well, actually . . .' She was about to explain the truth, but Sue stopped her with a gentle pinch.

'Don't spoil Miss P.'s trip down Memory Lane,' she whispered behind her hand into her friend's ear. 'I've already told Jill to cross out Peru. She's writing St Helena on the label!'